MW00770199

Palgrave Studies in US Elections

Series Editor
Luke Perry
Utica College
Utica, NY, USA

This Pivot series, established in collaboration with the Utica College Center of Public Affairs and Election Research, brings together cutting-edge work in US Politics focused on trends and issues surrounding local, state, and federal elections. Books in this series may cover but are not limited to topics such as voting behavior, campaign management, policy considerations, electoral social movements, and analysis of significant races. While welcoming all projects on US elections within and across all three levels of government, this series proceeds from the truism that all politics is fundamentally local. As such, we are especially interested in research on state and local elections such as mayoral races, gubernatorial races, and congressional elections, with particular focus on how state/local electoral trends influence national electoral politics, and vice versa. This series is open to any relevant scholar and all methodological approaches.

More information about this series at
http://www.palgrave.com/gp/series/16164

Andrew D. Green

From the Iowa Caucuses to the White House

Understanding Donald Trump's 2016 Electoral
Victory in Iowa

palgrave
macmillan

Andrew D. Green
Department of Political Science
Central College
Pella, IA, USA

Palgrave Studies in US Elections
ISBN 978-3-030-22498-1   ISBN 978-3-030-22499-8   (eBook)
https://doi.org/10.1007/978-3-030-22499-8

Cover illustration: Pattern © Melisa Hasan

This Palgrave Pivot imprint is published by the registered company Springer Nature Switzerland AG
The registered company address is: Gewerbestrasse 11, 6330 Cham, Switzerland

For my wife and sons,
Amber, Reese, and Reilly Green.

PREFACE

Iowa is considered "flyover" territory by many Americans. However, for politicos, Iowa provides excellent opportunities to observe and study elections and political institutions. While the state is more well known for the "retail politics" of the Iowa Caucuses, the state's status as a swing state, its significant share of "No Party" voters, its diverse "political geography", its non-partisan system of redistricting, its arduous process for amending the state constitution, and other political characteristics and institutions lead to interesting political outcomes, which should pique the curiosity of political scientists and politicos across the country. As interesting as Iowa politics is, little has been written about the state by political scientists. In short, Iowa politics is fascinating and justifies more attention from scholars.

The 2016 presidential election was a fascinating enterprise from start to finish in Iowa. Few expected Hillary Clinton to have a serious primary challenge. Even fewer expected Donald Trump to defeat 16 candidates to secure the Republican nomination for president. Both became a reality. Beginning with the Iowa Caucuses, Clinton was challenged by a 75-year-old self-proclaimed "Democratic Socialist" from Vermont named Bernie Sanders. Sanders caught fire in Iowa, and on caucus night, he essentially split the delegate count with Clinton. On the Republican side, except for Ted Cruz's significant campaign organization built to win the Republican Caucuses, Trump defeated the rest of the field of Republican candidates, which included seasoned campaigners like Jeb Bush, Chris Christie, Marco Rubio and Scott Walker. After securing the nomination of their respective political parties, both Clinton and Trump sent surrogates to the state, and they personally came back to campaign for Iowa's six

Electoral College votes. After a hard-fought campaign, Trump won the state by nearly 10%. His victory had down-ballot implications for political races all across the state.

Therefore, when given the chance to write a book on the 2016 campaign in Iowa, I jumped at the chance. Political scientists have examined the outcomes of presidential elections for decades, and more recently they have examined the outcome of the 2016 election using national-level data. However, one must ask: Are the findings of national-level studies applicable to the state, or are there other factors which shaped vote choice in 2016? The goal in writing this book was to develop a volume that provided readers an empirical frame to evaluate why Donald Trump was successful in Iowa. In other words, how did a billionaire businessman from Manhattan come to Iowa, a predominantly rural state, and find success? What explains his 10-point victory over Hillary Clinton? How do we explain the significant vote shifts that occurred between 2012 and 2016? The political science literature here is used as a theoretical guide to answer the aforementioned questions in an objective, evidence-based manner.

Additionally, it was important to develop a volume of interest to both scholars and teachers of electoral politics, as well as ensuring its accessibility and readability for observers of Iowa politics. To that end, a mixed-methods approach was utilized in developing the book. The qualitative data, collected through interviews with state political elites and an original survey of county party officials, paints a rich narrative about the 2016 campaign and its outcome in the state. The qualitative data is also used to inform the theoretical development of the quantitative statistical modeling at the county level and individual level. Every effort was made to explain the results of the statistical modeling in a substantive way that still makes sense to those who are not methodologically trained academics. Together, the qualitative and quantitative data effectively explains why Trump was so successful in courting Iowa voters in 2016, and these results create a potential roadmap for how the 2020 presidential campaign will proceed in Iowa.

After spending nearly a year developing and writing this book, I have a number of people to thank for their help and guidance. First, thank you to Luke Perry for including the volume in the new series "Palgrave Studies in US Elections." This book would not have become a reality without your support and interest.

To Michelle Chen, John Stegner, and the team at Palgrave Macmillan: Thank you for making this endeavor as easy as possible for a first-time author. Your assistance and responsiveness to inquiries is appreciated greatly.

Iowa's political culture certainly includes an emphasis on accessibility to candidates and public officials. However, political consultants and party officials in the state are also accessible to the people of Iowa. I want to thank Jeff Boeyink, Eric Branstad, Pete D'Alessandro, Jeff Kaufmann, David Kochel, Jeff Link, Andy McGuire, and Troy Price for their willingness to participate in elite interviews for the project. I also want to thank the Democratic and Republican county party officials who responded to the survey of county party officials.

I especially want to thank my colleagues at Central College for their assistance. To Mary Strey, Vice President for Academic Affairs, and the Faculty Development Committee: Thank you for your support of my sabbatical leave and R&D Grant, which were essential to developing the book. To Jenae Jenison, thank you for your help in setting up interviews with state political elites. To Kelly Taylor, thank you for processing the countless interlibrary loan requests I submitted for the project. To Jim Zaffiro, thank you for supporting the project and, as department chair, for helping me create space to complete the project. To Keith Yanner, thank you for reviewing chapter drafts and being a sounding board for ideas throughout the development of the project. Finally, to Josh Dolezal, Keith Jones, and Randy Renstrom, thank you for your advice and feedback at various stages of the project.

At Central College we are also fortunate to have talented students who are eager to work with faculty members on research projects. A big thank you goes to Kurt Sernett, a sophomore at Central College, who provided invaluable assistance during the development of the book.

Thank you to the following political science colleagues who provided important feedback on methodological questions and chapter drafts: Christopher Larimer, Dan Thomas, and Stacy Ulbig.

To my parents, Dennis and Mary Lu Green: Thank you for instilling in me a love of learning and reading, and for the impromptu "Grandma Camp" over spring break, which allowed me to focus a significant amount of time on writing.

Finally, I want to acknowledge my wife, Amber, and sons, Reese and Reilly. Maintaining balance in work-life and home-life is difficult when writing a book manuscript. Amber, thank you for your willingness to pick up some of the slack at home on top of the important work you do with students. Reese and Reilly, thank you for allowing me to go to work early or stay late from time to time while working on this project. Without your love and support, this book would not have been completed.

Pella, IA   Andrew D. Green

Praise for *From the Iowa Caucuses to the White House*

"We can finally stop all the speculation surrounding Donald Trump's surprise victory in Iowa in 2016. Andrew Green's insightful new book provides the first systematic and, importantly, data-driven look as to how Iowa, a state that twice voted for Obama, overwhelmingly voted for Trump. Anyone interested in understanding the shifting dynamics of presidential politics, where to look for answers in 2020, or why Iowa should still be considered a swing state needs to read this book."

—Christopher W. Larimer, *Professor of Political Science,*
University of Northern Iowa, USA

"Theories about why Donald Trump won the 2016 presidential election are common. In this book about the election in Iowa, Andrew Green brings evidence to the question. His in-depth analysis explores some of the common themes associated with the election, including change and the urban-rural divide, in order to explain the political conditions and campaign choices that led to a Trump victory."

—Julia Azari, *Associate Professor of Political Science, Marquette University, USA*

"In this impressive volume, Andrew Green takes a deep dive into Iowa's pivot to Trump in 2016. After detailing the enormity of the change, Green unpacks perspectives among Iowan political elites for local knowledge to inform plausible accounts on what happened, and then brings a series of regression analyses to bear in testing these accounts with county-wide and a sample of individual voters. The result is the definitive study of the Trump surprise—in a state going for Democrats in six of the last seven presidential elections."

—Dan Thomas, *Professor Emeritus, Wartburg College, USA*

CONTENTS

LIST OF FIGURES

LIST OF TABLES

CHAPTER 1

The 2016 Election in Iowa: An Introduction

I met the President for the first time ... April 8th, 2015, and I knew at
that meeting that he was going to be president. He has "it." My Dad
has "it." President Reagan had "it." President Clinton had "it." It's
just one of those things where they have a natural ability to really
connect with people.
—Eric Branstad, *Iowa State Political Director*
for Donald J. Trump for President

Abstract In this chapter, I contextualize the 2016 presidential election in Iowa, including a description of the election results statewide. Focusing on the literature written about Iowa politics, this chapter introduces the reader to the roots of competitive elections, which leads to the state being identified as a swing state. This chapter also focuses on the significant shift in candidate preference between Barack Obama's statewide victories in 2008 and 2012, and Donald Trump's statewide victory in 2016. It concludes with an outline for the remainder of the book, accompanied by a description of the remaining chapters.

Keywords Donald Trump • Hillary Clinton • Barack Obama • Swing state • Pivot counties

A. D. Green, *From the Iowa Caucuses to the White House,*
Palgrave Studies in US Elections,
https://doi.org/10.1007/978-3-030-22499-8_1

I remember the images like it was yesterday. I was driving on University Street in Pella, Iowa, on Saturday, January 23, 2016, on the campus of Central College. I saw the line extending from the exterior door of Douwstra Auditorium, down the campus walk, and then down the University Street sidewalk. There were vendors selling hats, buttons, and other memorabilia. The description above could describe a number of events held on college campuses every weekend. A concert. An appearance by a popular comedian. But what I was witnessing was no typical college campus event. What I saw was hundreds of Iowans who wanted to see Donald Trump, candidate for president. The Iowans in line that day filled Douwstra Auditorium to capacity and those who could not get into the auditorium were allowed into an overflow space in the banquet hall of an adjacent building. Mr. Trump's message that day was typical for his pre-Iowa Caucus rallies and would become the backbone of his message during the general election campaign. According to media reports, he talked about building the wall and that Mexico would pay for it. He discussed his support for the Keystone Pipeline and the Second Amendment. Ultimately, he reminded supporters in the room that his goal was to "Make America Great Again" (Presley 2016).

Donald Trump's ability to connect with people drove Iowans to attend rallies all over the State of Iowa during the pre-caucus period, and nine days after his rally in Pella, Trump finished second in the Iowa Caucuses to Senator Ted Cruz of Texas by a margin of 27.7% to 24.3% (WSJ News Graphics 2016). Trump carried 37 Iowa counties that evening and netted seven pledged delegates to the Republican National Convention (RNC).[1] After his close second-place finish in Iowa and a significant win in the New Hampshire primary the following week, Trump's campaign took off. While Cruz, Governor John Kasich of Ohio, and Senator Marco Rubio of Florida won a handful of primary contests throughout the primary season, Trump secured the nomination at the RNC in July 2016.

One week after giving his acceptance speech at the RNC in Cleveland, Donald Trump was back in Iowa campaigning for the presidency on July 28, 2016. On the same evening that Democratic nominee and former Secretary of State Hillary Clinton was giving her acceptance speech at the Democratic National Convention in Philadelphia, Trump held a campaign townhall at the Adler Theatre in Davenport, Iowa, followed by a campaign rally in Cedar Rapids (Appleman 2017). In addition to visits from running mate Governor Mike Pence of Indiana and other prominent surrogates for the Trump campaign, Donald Trump himself returned to Iowa six additional times throughout the fall campaign to interact with and engage supporters around the state. By the time November rolled around, Trump was well on his way to winning Iowa's six Electoral College votes. And indeed he did. On November 8, 2016, Donald Trump won the state over Hillary Clinton by nearly 10 points, securing the votes of 51.7% of Iowa voters (Iowa SOS 2016a).

Most observers of Iowa politics know that Trump won Iowa's six Electoral College votes by securing a majority of the popular vote in Iowa and that the typical county Trump won was primarily rural, white, lower income, and less educated. What many do not know is that the magnitude of Trump's victory was staggering. After Barack Obama won Iowa in 2008 and 2012, Trump won the popular vote in 93 of Iowa's 99 counties. Additionally, Trump flipped 32 counties that President Obama won in 2012. In these 32 counties, the difference between the margin of Obama's electoral victory in 2012 and the margin of Trump's victory in 2016 was not small. In fact, the average difference across the 32 counties was 27.6%, the difference in electoral margin was over 30% in 13 of the 32 counties, and the difference in electoral margin was over 40% in Howard County. These results lead to the following questions for this book: What explains Trump's electoral victory in Iowa in 2016? More specifically, what factors shaped support for Donald Trump among Iowa voters and explain the dramatic shift in county-level vote margins discussed above between 2012 and 2016? The goal of this project is to explain these shifts in electoral margin and ultimately identify the key factors which led to Trump's victory in the state.

The argument made in this book is that Donald Trump was the perfect candidate at the perfect time in Iowa. He entered the campaign as an "outsider" in a cycle that was identified as a "change" election. After he defeated 16 Republican candidates for the nomination, he entered the general election against Hillary Clinton, who was the epitome of the establishment. Clinton's "negatives" also helped fuel Trump's "change" narrative during the fall campaign. Furthermore, Trump had the special ability to communicate with Iowa's largest demographic cohort: White, working-class voters with conservative political views, especially regarding immigration and race. By winning over these white, working-class voters who had previously supported Obama, Trump was able to assemble a winning political coalition in the state and secure Iowa's six Electoral College votes on his way to the presidency.

The findings presented in the next three chapters make an important contribution to our understanding of presidential elections and Iowa politics for three reasons. First, while much has been written over the last few years about the 2016 presidential election, much of it utilizes national-level data, which does not allow for scholars and political observers to examine electoral outcomes on a state-by-state basis. The findings presented here, while taking into account major scholarship on presidential elections and the 2016 election, specifically, provide scholars and observers of Iowa politics a detailed explanation of support for Donald Trump in 2016 and the factors which shaped the significant shift in candidate preference between 2012 and 2016.

Second, Iowa is considered a swing state in presidential elections (Cillizza and Blake 2011; Hoffman and Larimer 2015). Over the last 10 elections dating back to 1980, the winner of the popular vote in Iowa was also the winner of the national popular vote in eight of those elections. The winning candidate in Iowa has been the Democratic nominee on six occasions (1988, 1992, 1996, 2000, 2008, 2012) and the Republican nominee on four occasions (1980, 1984, 2004, 2016). Iowa was also a unique case in 2016 since many voters, who had supported Barack Obama in 2008 and 2012, supported Donald Trump in 2016. Examining the shift in candidate preference will help scholars and practitioners not only gain a better understanding of the results in 2016, but it will also advance our knowledge of the relationship between candidate dynamics and electoral outcomes, particularly in swing states like Iowa.

Finally, this volume will contribute to our understanding of Iowa elections and politics. In attempting to defend Iowa's "first in the nation status," Lewis-Beck and Squire (2009) argue that Iowa is fairly representative of the nation as a whole, particularly in terms of economic characteristics. As a result, scholars and practitioners can learn from scholarship which focuses on the State of Iowa itself. There is a significant amount of scholarship focused on the Iowa Caucuses (e.g., Hull 2008; Squire 2008; Winebrenner and Goldford 2010; Redlawsk et al. 2011; Donovan et al. 2014; Darr 2019), and scholars have also studied Iowa election outcomes in gubernatorial elections (Larimer 2015), congressional elections (Hoffman and Larimer 2018), judicial retention elections (Clopton and Peters 2013), and the role of evangelical protestants in presidential elections (Racheter et al. 2003; Conger and Racheter 2006; Larimer and Hoffman 2018). The findings presented in the following chapters will enhance our understanding of voting behavior in Iowa by providing a comprehensive examination of how voters made choices in the 2016 presidential election.

1.1   THE ROOTS OF IOWA'S COMPETITIVE ELECTIONS

Politics in Iowa is deeply rooted in the cultural characteristics of moralism and individualism (Elazar 1984). In practice, this means that Iowans hold strong ties to their communities and believe government's purpose is to solve community problems. Iowans, on average, are patriotic and are proud of their state and local communities (Winebrenner and Goldford 2010). At the same time, Iowa's culture stresses the "primacy of the individual" in the marketplace as well as in public service. Ross (1990, 162–163) argues, the "moralistic atmosphere, with its elevated sense of individual responsibility, thrusts forward individuals who respond to the call of duty to help govern the community." As a result, "amateurism" in government is emphasized. Iowa's state legislature remains what political scientists call a "citizen's legislature"; and across Iowa, citizens volunteer to serve on municipal boards and commissions out of a sense of civic duty (Winebrenner and Goldford 2010).

Two other important political characteristics are born out of the moralistic and individualistic political culture of Iowa. First, Iowans generally prefer limited government and low taxes because of their preference for volunteerism in government and an emphasis on individual responsibility (Ross 1990; Winebrenner and Goldford 2010). This reality even extends to social issues where "Iowans tend to be fairly conservative, but they also are largely unwilling for government to impose standards of behavior on people" (Conger and Racheter 2006, 129). Second, the voting behavior of Iowans generates significant political competition in elections. Iowa's individualistic orientation to politics leads its voters to assess candidates as individuals, based upon the candidate's issue positions and their ability to solve problems (Ross 1990). This has created a "strong propensity for political independence," which leads to an increased level of split-ticket voting (Winebrenner and Goldford 2010, 16–17). The political independence of Iowans can be clearly seen by examining the number of registered "No Party" voters in the state immediately prior to the 2016 election. As of November 1, 2016, the Iowa Secretary of State (2016b) reported that of the nearly two million registered voters in the state, 34.8% were registered as No Party voters, 33.2% as Republicans, and 31.5% as Democrats. The political independence of Iowans can also be seen in election returns over the last 30 years. Many observers of Iowa politics often cite the fact that from 1985 until 2015, Iowa was represented in the U.S. Senate by Senator Tom Harkin, a Democrat, and Senator Charles Grassley, a Republican (Cillizza and Blake 2011; Larimer and Hoffman 2018). Split-ticket voting was also present in the 2016 election in the 2nd Congressional District, as

Donald Trump won the popular vote within the district by 4% and Representative Dave Loebsack, a Democrat, won the popular vote in his House race by 7% (Gregory 2017). Split-ticket voting was also on full display during the 2018 midterm elections when the Iowa U.S. House Delegation shifted from three Republicans and one Democrat to three Democrats and one Republican, all during the same election in which Republican Governor Kim Reynolds won her first full term as governor.

The competitiveness of elections in Iowa over time has led scholars and political pundits to identify Iowa as a "swing state" in presidential elections. Iowa was identified as a swing state in 2016 (Mahtesian 2016); and as Hoffman and Larimer (2015) point out, Iowa has been labeled as a swing state in every presidential election since the turn of the century. In addition to the political independence of Iowans, Hoffman and Larimer identify additional factors which explain why Iowa is a competitive, swing state in state-level elections. First, certain "structural" features of Iowa's political system, including Iowa's "first in the nation" caucuses, its nonpartisan system for redistricting, and voter registration laws, make it easy for voters to change their party registration prior to the Iowa Caucuses or a statewide primary election.

Additionally, Hoffman and Larimer (2015) argue that the "political geography" of Iowa plays a role in the competitiveness of Iowa elections (Fig. 1.1). Politically, Iowa differs significantly when comparing the east to the west and the rural to the urban.[2] The best description of western Iowa is rural and Republican. Western Iowa, outside of Sioux City in Woodbury County and Council Bluffs in Pottawattamie County, is very rural and has lost population since 2000. According to population estimates from the U.S. Census Bureau (2017), the average county population of western Iowa counties in 2016 was 18,664. Of the 45 counties in western Iowa, only nine counties experienced growth in population between 2000 and 2016. Western Iowa also leans Republican in terms of voter registration. In 2016, the share of voters registered as Republicans in western Iowa was 40.7% (IA SOS 2016b).[3] More than 60% of the residents in the four counties in extreme northwest Iowa (Lyon, O'Brien, Osceola, and Sioux) were registered Republicans and the share of voters who identify as Republicans exceeded 70% in Sioux County. The share of voters registered as Democrats in western Iowa was only 24.8% and registered "No Party" voters accounted for 34% of registered voters.

Much of eastern Iowa is also rural, but eastern Iowa is also the location of several urban areas in the state, including Cedar Falls and Waterloo in

Fig. 1.1 Map of Iowa counties. Map data from "maps" and "mapdata" packages in R

Black Hawk County; Cedar Rapids in Linn County; Iowa City in Johnson County; Bettendorf and Davenport in Scott County; and Dubuque in Dubuque County. The average population in 2016 for eastern Iowa counties was 33,880 residents. Although not to the same degree as western Iowa, many counties in eastern Iowa have also lost population since the 2000 census. U.S. Census Bureau (2017) estimates reveal that only 16 of the 49 counties in eastern Iowa have grown since 2000. Most of the counties which have experienced population growth are in the central portion of the region. The counties to the north along the Minnesota state line and to the south along the Missouri state line have all lost population since 2000 except Davis County, which has seen an estimated population growth of 3.7%.

Democrats enjoy some advantages in eastern Iowa, particularly in the urbanized areas of the region. The advantages in counties outside of urban areas, however, are not as significant as the advantages that Republicans enjoy in western Iowa. According to voter registration data from the Iowa Secretary of State (2016b), Democrats made up approximately 33% of all registered voters in eastern Iowa. The eastern Iowa county with the highest proportion of registered Democrats in 2016 was Johnson County

(47.8%), home to Iowa City and The University of Iowa. The difference in partisan advantage is visible when you compare the gap between the proportion of registered Republicans and Democrats across the two regions of the state. Whereas the gap between registered Republicans and registered Democrats in western Iowa was nearly 16%, the gap between registered Democrats and registered Republicans in eastern Iowa was around 3.5%. So, why the difference? More than likely, the reduced advantages that Democrats have in eastern Iowa are due to the sizable proportion of registered No Party voters in eastern Iowa. While the proportion of registered No Party voters in eastern Iowa was 36.5% in 2016, 12 counties in the region have proportions that exceed 40%—reaching as high as 45% for Howard and Jones Counties, and 47.6% for Buchanan County. In western Iowa, there were only five counties in which the percentage of registered No Party voters exceeded 40%, and the largest share was in Emmet County (43.4%).

1.2   The Shift in Candidate Preference Between 2008 and 2016

Senator Barack Obama's path to the presidency began in Iowa with the Iowa Democratic Caucus in 2008. In the months leading up to the 2008 campaign, most nationwide polls "indicated the Democratic race was between Hillary Clinton and everyone else" (Winebrenner and Goldford 2010, 309). In what would ultimately become a six-candidate race, Obama built a grassroots organization which relied heavily on the enthusiasm of young voters and a significant number of Iowans who had never participated in the Iowa Caucuses. On caucus night, which Obama has since called "my favorite night of my entire political career" (Liddell-Westefeld 2018), Obama won the Iowa Democratic Caucus with 37.6% of the state delegate equivalent (DMR n.d.). Senator John Edwards of North Carolina and Clinton finished second and third with 29.8% and 29.5%, respectively. Turnout was extremely high. Approximately 240,000 Iowans participated in Democratic Caucuses all over the state.

After winning the Iowa Democratic Caucus in January, Obama won a resounding victory in Iowa during the 2008 presidential general election. Obama won the popular vote 53.7% to 44.2% over Senator John McCain of Arizona (IA SOS 2008). Obama won 53 of Iowa's 99 counties. His core support was found not only in urban areas but also in more rural counties across the state. He won all the counties in the Mississippi River

Valley and along the northern state line with Minnesota from Allamakee County in northeast Iowa to Emmet County in north-central Iowa. Obama even won counties in the central portion of western Iowa, including Audubon, Carroll, Crawford, and Greene Counties, as well as three counties in southwestern Iowa (Adams, Clarke, and Union). In doing so, Obama's vote total exceeded that of every presidential candidate in Iowa history (Beaumont 2008).

In 2012, President Obama once again won the State of Iowa's six Electoral College votes. After personally visiting the state 13 times beginning in April 2012 (Appleman 2012), Obama ended his presidential campaign with a rally in the East Village of Des Moines with his wife, Michelle, and rock legend Bruce Springsteen. David Nakamura (2012) of *The Washington Post* said the "decision to bid farewell to the campaign trail with a nighttime appearance in Des Moines's historic East Village was as symbolic as it was strategic." The event was symbolic in the sense that Obama was coming back to Iowa for one more rally, just blocks from the location of his first 2008 field office and in the state that propelled him forward toward the nomination. It was strategic in that Iowa was a swing state he needed to win. After winning the 2008 campaign with a message of "Hope" and "Change," Obama acknowledged his understanding of the fact that some of his supporters were "frustrated at the pace of change" (Obama 2012). His comments suggested two political realities. One, that some "change" voters from the 2008 election cycle were upset with the speed in which change was being delivered and, as a result, were considering a vote for his opponent, Governor Mitt Romney. And two, that politically he understood the need to maintain those 2008 "change" voters in his political coalition to win Iowa in 2012.

President Obama did indeed win Iowa in 2012, but the margins were much closer than in his 2008 victory. Obama won the state with 51.7% of the vote to Romney's 46% (IA SOS 2012). While Obama's raw vote only dropped by approximately 6400 votes statewide, Romney significantly overperformed John McCain, winning about 50,000 more votes statewide than the 2008 Republican nominee. In doing so, Romney won 61 Iowa counties while flipping 16 counties that Obama had won in 2008. Most of the counties Romney flipped were in western Iowa, but he also flipped several counties in northern Iowa along the Minnesota border and even in eastern Iowa (Benton, Delaware, and Iowa Counties). Obama did flip one county that he lost to McCain in 2008: Woodbury County. The margin in both contests was razor thin. McCain won Woodbury County by less than a percentage point (49.6%-49.1%) in 2008 (IA SOS 2008) and Obama defeated Romney in Woodbury County by about one percentage point in 2012 (50.5%-49.5%).

The erosion of the Obama coalition continued into the 2016 cycle. Hillary Clinton, whom Republicans claimed was "running for Obama's third term" (McCaskill 2016), "came to be seen as establishment and dishonest in a year when a plurality of voters wanted change" (Wasserman 2017).[4] Conversely, Donald Trump was viewed by many Iowans as the candidate who would not forget rural and working-class voters once he was in the White House. During the summer of 2016, political experts in the state argued that Trump's keys to victory were twofold: (1) Keep Republican base voters, particularly rural voters, in line and turn them out to vote; and (2) Lockdown the votes of the working-class, many of whom voted for Obama in 2008 and 2012 (Noble 2016b). For Clinton, experts argued that she needed to focus "on women, Latinos, and voters in the suburbs surrounding Iowa's major cities" (Noble 2016a). Additionally, experts argued that Clinton could seek out votes in rural Iowa by emphasizing her support for wind energy and ethanol. By doing so, she could prevent Trump from running up the score in rural Iowa and create a path for herself to win statewide.

On Election Day, support for Trump was overwhelming. He won the statewide two-party vote 50.7% to Clinton's 41.3% (IA SOS 2016a). He won 93 of Iowa's 99 counties; and in doing so, flipped 32 counties that Obama had won in 2012. Figure 1.2 shows counties which were flipped by Trump in 2016 known as "pivot counties." The light gray color represents counties won by Romney in 2012 and Trump in 2016, or by Obama in 2012 and Clinton in 2016. The dark gray shaded counties are counties won by Obama in 2012 and by Trump in 2016. Notice that only 5 of the 32 pivot counties are in western Iowa, which should not be surprising based upon what we know about Romney's 2012 performance in the region. The vast majority of the pivot counties are in eastern Iowa, particularly along the northern border of the state and in the Mississippi River Valley, where there are significant pockets of working-class voters the Trump campaign was targeting.

Trump also significantly overperformed Mitt Romney's 2012 vote total. In fact, he overperformed Romney by more than 70,000 votes statewide (IA SOS 2012, 2016a). Figure 1.3 displays the breakdown of Trump's overperformance of Romney across Iowa's 99 counties. In the figure, the darker the shade of gray, the larger the overperformance of Mitt

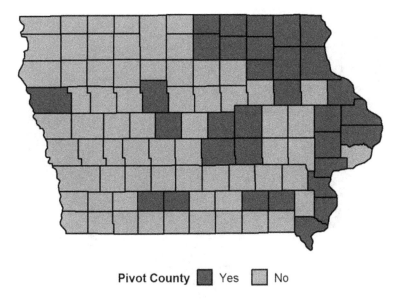

Pivot County ■ Yes ■ No

Fig. 1.2 Pivot counties in Iowa, 2016. Map data from "maps" and "mapdata" packages in R

Romney's 2012 two-party vote share in the county. Note that Trump's overperformance of Romney failed to exceed 5% in only six counties. Four of the six counties are urban counties Clinton won, including Johnson, Linn, Polk, and Story Counties. Also note that Trump overperformed Romney in two additional counties that Clinton won: Black Hawk and Scott. It is also clear that while Trump overperformed Romney across the state, Trump fared very well in the rural counties along the Missouri border and in several counties in northeast Iowa, including Howard County where his overperformance of Romney was 21.6%.

Clinton, on the other hand, only won Iowa's six urban counties (Black Hawk, Johnson, Linn, Polk, Scott, and Story Counties). She lost the suburban counties of Dallas and Warren, which surround the Des Moines Metro. In terms of her raw vote, she underperformed Obama's 2012 vote total by nearly 170,000 votes (IA SOS 2012, 2016a). Perhaps more significantly, one can recognize her underperformance of Obama in the six counties that she did win. She actually underperformed Obama by more than 7500 votes in Black Hawk County, more than 9600 votes in Linn

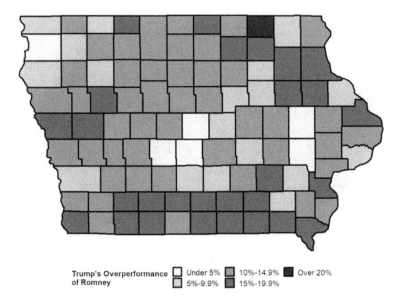

Fig. 1.3 Donald Trump's two-party vote share in 2016 versus Mitt Romney's two-party vote share in 2012. Map data from "maps" and "mapdata" packages in R

County, more than 8600 votes in Polk County, and more than 10,000 votes in Scott County. Her performance in Johnson and Story Counties was better, but she still underperformed Obama by more than 400 votes in each county. All told, her underperformance of Barack Obama in those six counties totaled 37,056 votes, which accounted for more than 20% of her total underperformance statewide.

Two other trends stood out in the macro-level data. One was the significant advantage that Trump had on Election Day. The Clinton campaign and the Iowa Democratic Party were able to bank a 61,000 vote lead during the early voting period.[5] Nonetheless, Trump overcame the 61,000 vote deficit from early voting and won the vote on Election Day by over 200,000 votes. Second, there was the significant increase in votes for minor party candidates in 2016 (IA SOS 2016a). From 2012 to 2016, support for the Constitution Party's candidate increased from around 3000 votes in 2012 to over 5300 votes in 2016. Jill Stein, candidate for the Green Party in both 2012 and 2016, saw her vote total increase by nearly 8000 votes statewide. Governor Gary Johnson, candidate for the

Libertarian Party in both 2012 and 2016, saw his vote share increase by over 46,000 votes statewide. Similarly, the number of write-in votes increased from 7442 in 2012 to 17,746 in 2016.

At the individual-level, Trump did very well with the key constituencies noted by Noble (2016a, b) while Clinton did not. According to exit polls of Iowa voters, Trump was able to keep the Republican base and evangelical Christians in the coalition, securing 90% of the Republican vote and 70% of evangelical Christians (Exit Polls 2016). He won 63% of the vote in rural areas of the state. And finally, Trump won 67% of voters who said they were dissatisfied with or angry at the federal government, 71% of voters who perceived the condition of the national economy as poor, and 82% of voters who perceived their personal financial conditions as "worse today" versus one year prior.

Clinton, on the other hand, did not do as well with key constituencies. Exit polls revealed that, while she indeed won a majority of the votes of Iowa women (51%), she only carried the vote of white women by 3% (49%-46%) and the vote of college-educated women by 11% (52%-41%) (Exit Polls 2016). In fact, white women without college degrees favored Trump 49% to 47%; and married women, who made up more than a third of exit poll respondents, favored Trump 50% to 45%. Clinton also needed to maximize her vote margins in the urban and suburban areas of the state, but she underperformed President Obama in the urban areas of the state by 11% (68% for Obama in 2012 versus 57% for Clinton in 2016) and actually lost the popular vote of suburban voters by 9% (51%-42%). She also underperformed Obama in rural Iowa. In 2016, she lost the rural vote by 30% (63%-33%); but in 2012, Obama only lost the rural vote 52%-46% or by a six-point margin (Exit Polls 2012). Clinton did win the Latino/Latina vote by 37% (63%-26%), but Latinos and Latinas only represented 5% of exit poll respondents statewide at the time.

1.3   PLAN FOR THE BOOK

The remainder of this book is organized as follows. In Chap. 2, I present an analysis of an original qualitative dataset collected from November 2018 through February 2019. The dataset includes responses to a survey from Iowa Democratic and Republican county party officials across the state as well as interview data from eight interviews conducted with statewide party leaders and political consultants. The analysis identifies and describes the five major themes from the campaign in the qualitative data: (1) The enthusiasm gap; (2) Antipathy toward Hillary Clinton; (3) Differences in campaign organization and elite support; (4) The significance of the rural–urban divide; and (5) 2016 was a "change" election.

Chapters 3 and 4 examine the results of the 2016 presidential election in Iowa utilizing county-level and individual-level data. In Chap. 3, there is a discussion of the academic literature oriented toward presidential elections, Iowa elections, and the 2016 election. The literature is used to theoretically develop models of vote choice using county-level data in Chap. 3 and individual-level data in Chap. 4 to determine if indeed the major findings in the literature from the 2016 presidential election are generalizable to Iowa. County-level models reveal that Trump was able to build a winning coalition between Republican and evangelical voters, and he was able to secure the votes of white, working-class voters across the state. County-level models also indicate that Trump's improved performance over Mitt Romney in 2012 was driven by white, working-class voters as well, not by the core constituencies of the Republican base. The individual-level findings of Chap. 4 demonstrate that the 2016 election was not driven solely by white, working-class support. Rather, support for Donald Trump was driven by partisanship, attitudes regarding President Obama's performance, and hardline positions on immigration, not by educational attainment. Additionally, educational attainment did not drive vote switching in 2016 either. Vote switching—casting a vote for Obama or a third-party candidate in 2012 and then for Trump in 2016—was both a function of voters' approval of Obama's performance as president and their attitudes about race.

In the final chapter of this book, the major findings of the book are discussed and placed in the context of the academic literature on past presidential elections, Iowa elections, and the 2016 presidential election. A discussion of the book's major implications for the literature is also presented. This chapter concludes with a discussion regarding what we can expect as the 2020 election cycle continues. For example, how do the lessons learned from the 2016 race in Iowa impact how we view the 2020 race here as well? What should we expect to see in terms of candidate emergence on both sides of the political spectrum leading up to the Iowa Caucuses? What should we expect to see in terms of candidate strategy during the nominating stage, and ultimately, during the general election season?

NOTES

1. Although ultimately all 30 delegates from Iowa to the RNC voted for Donald Trump. See Rosenthal (2016).
2. Western Iowa is defined as counties west of Interstate 35 not including the five counties in the Des Moines Metropolitan Statistical Area (Dallas, Guthrie, Madison, Polk, and Warren). The remaining counties to the east of Interstate 35 are defined as Eastern Iowa.
3. All voter registration data presented here focuses on voters classified by the Iowa Secretary of State's office as "Active" voters. "Inactive" voters were excluded.
4. 2016 exit polls revealed that 43% of Iowa voters believed that "can bring change" was the most important candidate quality (Exit Polls 2016).
5. In 2012, after the early vote was counted Obama had a 137,000 vote advantage (IA SOS 2012, 2016a).

REFERENCES

Appleman, Eric M. 2012. Obama-Biden Iowa Visits. http://www.p2012.org/obama/obamaiavisits12.html.

———. 2017. Trump-Pence Iowa Visits. http://www.p2016.org/trump/trumpiavisits16.html.

Beaumont, Thomas. 2008. Iowans There for Obama at Race's Start and Finish. *Des Moines Register*, November 5. ProQuest.

Cillizza, Chris, and Aaron Blake. 2011. Is Iowa a Swing State? *The Fix* (blog). *Washington Post*, August 16. https://www.washingtonpost.com/blogs/the-fix/post/is-iowa-a-swing-state/2011/08/15/gIQAHG6tIJ_blog.html?utm_term=.1725fc95d2f0.

Clopton, Andrew J., and C. Scott Peters. 2013. Justices Denied: A County-Level Analysis of the 2010 Iowa Supreme Court Retention Election. *Justice System Journal* 34 (3): 321–344. https://doi.org/10.1080/00982 61X.2013.10768043.

Conger, Kimberly H., and Donald Racheter. 2006. Iowa: In the Heart of Bush Country. In *The Values Campaign? The Christian Right and the 2004 Elections*, ed. John C. Green, Mark J. Rozell, and Clyde Wilcox, 128–142. Washington, DC: Georgetown University Press.

Darr, Joshua P. 2019. Earning Iowa: Local Newspapers and the Invisible Primary. *Social Science Quarterly* 100 (1): 320–327. https://doi.org/10.1111/ssqu.12565.

Des Moines Register. n.d. Iowa Caucuses: Caucus History. Accessed February 25, 2019. https://data.desmoinesregister.com/iowa-caucus/history/index.php#2008/dem.

Donovan, Todd, David Redlawsk, and Caroline Tolbert. 2014. The 2012 Iowa Republican Caucus and Its Effects on the Presidential Nomination Contest. *Presidential Studies Quarterly* 44 (3): 447–466.

Elazar, Daniel J. 1984. *American Federalism: A View from the States.* 3rd ed. New York: Holt Rinehart.

Exit Polls. 2012. Exit Polls: Iowa President. Last Modified December 10, 2012. http://www.cnn.com/election/2012/results/state/IA/president/.

———. 2016. Exit Polls: Iowa President. Last Modified November 23, 2016. https://www.cnn.com/election/2016/results/exit-polls/iowa/president.

Gregory, Grant. 2017. How Dave Loebsack Beat the Trump Bump. *Iowa Starting Line,* January 12. https://iowastartingline.com/2017/01/12/dave-loeb-sack-beat-trump-bump/.

Hoffman, Donna R., and Christopher W. Larimer. 2015. Battleground Iowa: Swing State Extraordinaire. In *Presidential Swing States: Why Only Ten Matter,* ed. Stacey Hunter Hecht and David Schultz, 265–289. Lanham, MD: Lexington Books.

———. 2018. Iowa First Congressional District: Anomaly or New Normal? In *The Roads to Congress 2016: American Elections in a Divided Landscape,* ed. Sean D. Foreman and Marcia L. Godwin, 139–153. New York: Palgrave Macmillan.

Hull, Christopher C. 2008. *Grassroots Rules: How the Iowa Caucus Helps Elect American Presidents.* Stanford: Stanford University Press.

Iowa Secretary of State (IA SOS). 2008. State of Iowa Official Canvass Summary, November 4, 2008 General Election. https://sos.iowa.gov/elections/pdf/2008/OfficialCanvass2008General.pdf.

———. 2012. 2012 General Election Canvass Summary. https://sos.iowa.gov/elections/pdf/2012/general/canvsummary.pdf.

———. 2016a. 2016 General Election Canvass Summary. https://sos.iowa.gov/elections/pdf/2016/primary/canvsummary.pdf.

———. 2016b. State of Iowa Voter Registration Totals: County (11/1/2016). https://sos.iowa.gov/elections/pdf/VRStatsArchive/2016/CoNov16.pdf.

Larimer, Christopher W. 2015. *Gubernatorial Stability in Iowa: A Stranglehold on Power.* New York: Palgrave Macmillan.

Larimer, Christopher W., and Donna R. Hoffman. 2018. Iowa: The Religious Right as Sometime Republican Kingmaker. In *God at the Grassroots 2016: The Christian Right in American Politics,* ed. Mark J. Rozell and Clyde Wilcox, 49–67. Lanham, MD: Rowman & Littlefield.

Lewis-Beck, Michael S., and Peverill Squire. 2009. Iowa: The Most Representative State? *PS: Political Science & Politics* 42 (1): 39–44. https://doi.org/10.1017/S1049096509090039.

Liddell-Westefeld, Chris. 2018. They Said This Day Would Never Come. *Crooked Media,* January 3. https://crooked.com/articles/said-day-never-come/.

Mahtesian, Charlie. 2016. What Are the Swing States in 2016? *Battleground States Project* (blog), *Politico,* June 15. https://www.politico.com/blogs/swing-states-2016-election/2016/06/what-are-the-swing-states-in-2016-list-224327.

McCaskill, Nolan D. 2016. Obama: I Could Have Won a Third Term. *Politico*, December 26. https://www.politico.com/story/2016/12/barack-obama-axelrod-third-term-hope-change-232969.

Nakamura, David. 2012. A Nostalgic Obama Returns to Iowa for the End of His Last Campaign. *Washington Post*, November 6. ProQuest.

Noble, Jason. 2016a. Clinton's Path to Win Runs Through Suburbs. *Des Moines Register*, August 10. ProQuest.

———. 2016b. To Win Iowa, Trump Must Woo Unhappy Workers. *Des Moines Register*, August 11. ProQuest.

Obama, Barack. 2012. Remarks by the First Lady and the President at Final Campaign Rally – Des Moines, IA. Accessed February 26, 2019. https://obamawhitehouse.archives.gov/the-press-office/2012/11/06/remarks-first-lady-and-president-final-campaign-rally-des-moines-ia.

Presley, Nicole. 2016. Trump Stumps in Pella. *Pella Chronicle*, January 25. https://www.pellachronicle.com/news/trump-stumps-in-pella/article_151e921e-c385-11e5-a01a-97260fl2d9e4.html.

Racheter, Donald P., Lyman A. Kellstedt, and John C. Green. 2003. Iowa: Crucible of the Christian Right. In *The Christian Right in American Politics: Marching to the Millennium*, ed. John C. Green, Mark J. Rozell, and Clyde Wilcox, 121–144. Washington, DC: Georgetown University Press.

Redlawsk, David P., Caroline J. Tolbert, and Todd Donovan. 2011. *Why Iowa? How Caucuses and Sequential Elections Improve the Presidential Nominating Process*. Chicago: University of Chicago Press.

Rosenthal, Eric. 2016. All Iowa Republican National Delegates Will Vote for Donald Trump. *Cedar Rapids Gazette*, June 1. https://www.thegazette.com/subject/opinion/guest-columnists/all-iowa-republican-national-delegates-will-vote-for-donald-trump-20160601.

Ross, Robert. 1990. Governance and Politics in Iowa Communities. In *Issues in Iowa Politics*, ed. Lee Ann Osbun and Steffen W. Schmidt, 160–182. Ames, IA: Iowa State University Press.

Squire, Peverill. 2008. The Iowa Caucuses, 1972–2008: A Eulogy. *The Forum* 5 (4): 1–9. https://doi.org/10.2202/1540-8884.1212.

U.S. Census Bureau. 2017. Annual Estimates of the Resident Population: April 1, 2010 to July 1, 2016. Released March 2017.

Wasserman, David. 2017. The One County in America That Voted in a Landslide for Both Trump and Obama. *FiveThirtyEight*, November 9. https://fivethirtyeight.com/features/the-one-county-in-america-that-voted-in-a-landslide-for-both-trump-and-obama/.

Winebrenner, Hugh, and Dennis J. Goldford. 2010. *The Iowa Precinct Caucuses: The Making of a Media Event*. 3rd ed. Iowa City: The University of Iowa Press.

WSJ News Graphics. 2016. Results from the 2016 Iowa Caucus. Last Modified February 2, 2016. http://graphics.wsj.com/elections/2016/iowa-caucus-results/.

CHAPTER 2

Viewing the 2016 Presidential Campaign Through the Lens of Iowa Political Elites

*Two guys were coming up ... I forget which union they were a part of,
they were leaving, and I walked up to them, I had to. I said, "I'm the
chairman of the Republican Party" and they said, "We're Democrats."
I said, "Well, first thing I'm going to tell you is welcome, you are more
than welcome here." I said, "I gotta ask you, ...
why are you here? I mean we're glad you are here, but why are you here?"
"He's the only one that will say what's on his mind." I really think,
even though that's just two people, one day, and they cared enough about it
to show up at this rally, I really think that was replayed and
I think it crossed party lines, and I think it crossed ideological lines,
and I think it tapped into that long time historic trend, and I think he had
kind of a perfect storm going there.*
—Jeff Kaufmann, *Chairman of the Republican Party of Iowa*

Abstract In this chapter, I present a qualitative analysis of an original dataset collected through interviews of Iowa political elites and a survey of county party officials. After providing the reader with a description of the methods used to collect the data, I identify five major themes from the 2016 presidential campaign as viewed by Iowa's state and local political elites, including: (1) the enthusiasm gap; (2) antipathy toward Hillary Clinton; (3) differences in campaign organization and elite support; (4) the significance of the rural–urban divide; and (5) 2016 being a "change" election.

© The Author(s) 2020   19
A. D. Green, *From the Iowa Caucuses to the White House,*
Palgrave Studies in US Elections,
https://doi.org/10.1007/978-3-030-22499-8_2

Keywords Qualitative analysis • Iowa political elites • Rural–Urban divide • Change election

The "perfect storm." An appropriate metaphor for how the 2016 presidential campaign played out in the State of Iowa. In the epigraph above, Jeff Kaufmann, the Chairman of the Republican Party of Iowa, is talking about an encounter he had with two union Democrats at a Trump rally in Cedar Rapids, Iowa, in late July 2016 (Kaufmann 2019). The "long-time historic trend" he is referring to is the "strain of populism" that has been observed in Iowa over the state's history. While he was specifically referencing populism above, there were other factors which helped shape the perfect storm in 2016. The built up antipathy toward Hillary Clinton. A fracture in the Democratic electorate that was exposed during the primary season. A significant enthusiasm gap between Democrats and Republicans. Significant differences in "elite support." An electorate that desired change from the status quo. And the growing political divide between rural Iowa and urban Iowa. All these forces came together in the fall of 2016 and fueled voter support for Donald Trump and ultimately led to his victory in the state.

The full story of Trump's victory in Iowa cannot be told by focusing on quantitative modeling of county-level or individual-level data alone. As a result, a mixed-methods approach is utilized over the next three chapters. In order to fully tell the story, I felt it was important to allow state and local party elites to weigh in on what transpired not only statewide but also in counties all over the state. This decision was important for a couple of reasons: (1) because perceptions and attitudes regarding the campaign may differ between the state and local level; and (2) because campaign dynamics could have differed across the various regions of the state. Their attitudes and perceptions were aggregated into a qualitative dataset based upon a series of interviews with state party leaders and consultants, and an original survey of county party chairs from Iowa's 99 counties. The qualitative data will be used throughout this chapter to identify major themes from the 2016 election and will also be used in the next two chapters to aid in the theoretical development of the quantitative models presented in each chapter.

The remainder of this chapter is laid out as follows. First, a description of the survey and interview methods is presented, including a discussion of how participants were selected and the methods through which the qualitative data was collected. After the discussion of methods, a detailed description of the qualitative data is presented. The description focuses on major themes identified across the interviewees but also the respondents to the original survey. At the end of this chapter, the genesis of the "perfect storm" will be clear: For many Iowa voters, Donald Trump was the perfect candidate at the perfect time.

2.1   METHODS AND DATA

The survey of county party officials consisted of a 25–26 item questionnaire delivered primarily online through Qualtrics. After spending a considerable amount of time reviewing popular press accounts of the 2016 election, as well as public and academic scholarship written to date on 2016, the survey instrument was created during the fall of 2018. The base questionnaire included nine open-ended questions, which were nearly identical to the interview questions described in the next section below, and 16 closed-ended items that included either yes/no options or Likert scales. In developing the survey, the goal was to learn more about the "macrolevel" perceptions and attitudes regarding the campaign in Iowa, including major determinants of vote switching at the county level, descriptions of the campaign organizations and grassroots support, and the impacts of the rural–urban divide on vote choice. Additionally, I was interested in collecting data on "microlevel" factors which shaped the 2016 outcome, including a specific focus on registered "No Party" voters (i.e., Independents), the importance of issues to voters in their home counties, and the importance of major campaign events, both in Iowa and nationally, to voters in their counties. Republican county party officials received the base questionnaire. Democratic county party officials received a modified questionnaire, which consisted of the base questionnaire along with an additional open-ended item probing into the presence of organized or unorganized opposition to Hillary Clinton from caucus supporters of Bernie Sanders.[1]

To facilitate the online delivery of the survey to the 198 county party chairs, the contact information, including name, mailing address, and email address, for party chairs was collected from the campaign report filed by the party's Central Committee in each Iowa county immediately prior to the 2016 election.[2] Five county party chairs did not have email addresses on file, so only their mail address was collected. In one case, the county party chair from the 2016 election cycle was deceased, so the current county party chair's contact information was collected. In mid-November, a hard-copy letter was mailed to each county party chair to notify them of their selection to participate in the survey and to verify their email address.[3] The letter also notified them that they would receive an automated email from Qualtrics in the next week or so and that it was safe to click on the link to access the survey. Additionally, the letter told them to notify me if the chair preferred to receive a hard-copy of the survey, or if the chair was not interested in participating, to suggest another member of the county's Central Committee to contact. Two party chairs contacted me to opt out of the online version and complete a hard-copy version and several chairs suggested contacting another member of the county's Central Committee to complete the survey.

On November 30, 2018, the survey was distributed. County party chairs with a valid email address on file received an email with a unique link to access and complete the survey. For the seven party chairs with no email address, a hard-copy of the survey including a postage-paid return envelope was distributed via the USPS. Reminder email messages were sent periodically during December 2018 and January 2019 from Qualtrics to the officials who had not yet completed the survey. By mid-February 2019, four of the seven chairs who had received the hard-copy survey in the mail returned a completed survey. Eighty-one of the 191 party chairs who received the electronic invitation clicked into the site. Two immediately opted out of the survey via the informed consent item. Eleven respondents consented to participate in the survey but did not provide responses to a single survey item. The remaining 68 respondents provided responses to some or all the survey items for an overall response rate of 36.4%, when including the four hard-copy submissions. Responses were received from at least one-party official from 58 of Iowa's 99 counties, and responses were received from a county party official from both parties for 10 counties. In terms of geographic distribution, 30.9% of respondents were from northeast Iowa, 26.5% from northwest Iowa, 19.1% from southwest Iowa, 13.2% from southeast Iowa, and 10.3% from central Iowa.[4] Forty-two of the 68 respondents are Democrats and 26 are Republicans.

The qualitative data analyzed below also includes data from eight interviews completed with statewide political elites between December 2018 and February 2019. I was interested in interviewing political elites who were intimately involved in the general election campaign in 2016. Additionally, I was interested in interviewing political elites who have experience running campaigns in Iowa and therefore understand the political dynamics of the state. Based upon the aforementioned parameters, I identified eight individuals, four Democrats and four Republicans, to interview. Seven of the eight individuals were sent a hard-copy letter through the mail, requesting an opportunity to interview them for the project. The eighth was contacted via email because no mailing address was made available for contacting the individual. After a series of follow-up emails with each individual, all interviews were scheduled and conducted by February 2019. The interviewees included (in order of completion):

- Eric Branstad, Iowa State Director for Donald J. Trump for President
- Jeff Boeyink, Campaign Manager for Governor Terry Branstad's 2010 election campaign and Governor Branstad's Chief of Staff from 2010 to 2013
- Andy McGuire, former Chairwoman of the Iowa Democratic Party
- David Kochel, Senior Strategist for Jeb Bush's 2016 Presidential Campaign
- Pete D'Alessandro, Campaign Coordinator for Bernie Sanders's Caucus Campaign
- Jeff Link, Campaign Manager for Senator Tom Harkin's 1996 and 2002 re-election campaigns, Iowa State Director for Al Gore's 2000 Caucus Campaign, and Deputy Director for Paid Media for Barack Obama's 2008 Presidential Campaign
- Jeff Kaufmann, Chairman of the Republican Party of Iowa
- Troy Price, Senior Advisor in Iowa for Hillary for America and current Chairman of the Iowa Democratic Party

A base interview schedule was created in November 2018 for use in each interview. Similar to the approach used in creating the survey described above, questions probed into both macrolevel perceptions and attitudes about the 2016 campaign and microlevel factors which shaped the outcome. As necessary, follow-up questions were offered to clarify or further probe into previous responses. Each interviewee signed an informed consent statement, which clarified how the interview data could be used for the project. Seven of the eight interviews were completed face to face and the eighth interview was completed over the phone. Interviews ranged from a little more than 29 minutes to just over 50 minutes in length. Each interview was recorded using a digital voice recorder and a time-stamped index of each interview was created afterward. None of the interviews were transcribed.

The themes discussed below were identified through a careful review of the interview recordings and answers to both the open-ended and closed-ended survey questions. I started the process by reviewing the eight interview recordings, noting prevalent themes across the interviews. Each theme was recorded in a separate document from the interview index forms, including specific references to portions of each interview.[5] After completing the review of the interview recordings, I moved on to reviewing the open-ended and closed-ended survey items. While doing so, I created a separate document once again, noting prevalent themes across responses to various questions. After reviewing the survey data, I began to compare the two documents while recognizing consistencies across both the interviews and survey responses, which suggest that both state political elites and county political elites agree on certain themes. In other areas, there is evidence that disputes certain themes. In those cases, the evidence was noted and is discussed as a part of the overall theme below.

2.2   THEME #1: THE ENTHUSIASM GAP

At the national level, the initial signs of an enthusiasm gap date back to late 2015 as the primary field shaped up on both sides. According to multiple polls, Republican voters were much more likely to be excited to vote for president in the upcoming year than Democratic voters (Shepard 2015). Democratic elites downplayed the gap as a function of the competitive primary on the GOP side; and once a nominee was selected to run against Clinton, enthusiasm among Democrats would increase. Republican pollsters agreed in part. They knew that the gap would narrow as the fall campaign approached, but they also "cautioned that Democrats may never be truly pumped for Clinton's candidacy." And they were right. According to ABC News/*Washington Post* polling data in the seven weeks prior to the 2016 election, strong enthusiasm among Clinton voters trailed that of Trump voters in all but one poll (Langer 2016). One week before Election Day, strong enthusiasm among Trump voters reached 53%, while strong enthusiasm among Clinton voters dropped to 45%, an 8% enthusiasm gap.

It is important to understand the enthusiasm gap in elections because enthusiasm can drive voter turnout in an election. When evaluating polling data, Jeff Boeyink (2018) first looks for an "enthusiasm gap between the parties" because the presence of an enthusiasm gap "is the best predictor of turnout than just about anything." No publicly available polling data measured enthusiasm among Iowa voters in the lead up to the November 2016 election; however, early vote returns may have been an initial sign of lower enthusiasm for Democratic voters. While in mid-October of 2016 Democratic voters had requested and submitted more early ballots than Republicans, the total number of requests from Democrats was down by nearly 38,000 ballots, and the number of submitted ballots was down by nearly 32,000 from 2012 (Noble 2016b). When evaluating the level of enthusiasm for the two 2016 candidates using the interview and survey data collected for this project, one thing is clear: Iowa political elites, both at the state and county level, perceived a significant enthusiasm gap between Democratic and Republican voters during the 2016 election cycle.

Many Democratic respondents to the survey noted a lack of enthusiasm for Hillary Clinton's candidacy during the 2016 campaign. Andy McGuire (2018) and Troy Price (2019) both indicated during separate interviews that 2016 lacked enthusiasm, excitement, and energy, especially when compared to the 2008 and 2012 Obama campaigns. While it is plausible that the lack of enthusiasm was driven by antipathy toward Clinton, Price speculates that it may have been a function of messaging. He discussed the campaign's focus on rebuilding "the Obama coalition, which was working-class voters, African Americans, ... and minorities and Latinos." Unlike Obama's ability to develop a "unified message" across the aforementioned groups, he believes Clinton's campaign was unable to deliver that unifying message; as a result, the message coming from the campaign did not resonate with Iowa voters.

While neither the interview schedule nor the survey included items specific to the existence of an enthusiasm gap, the lack of enthusiasm for Clinton's campaign is borne out in three different ways across a series of items, both in the interview data and in the survey. First, several Democratic respondents indicated that it was very difficult to recruit local volunteers during the campaign. Whether it was recruiting to staff phone banks or canvas door to door, there was a real resistance to volunteering for the Democratic nominee. One Democratic respondent from northwest Iowa went as far as to say that they had to "beg people to help." It was also telling that only one Democratic respondent to the survey indicated it was easy to recruit "a good number of local volunteers" and one other Democratic respondent said there were "a lot of volunteers" in the county. In his interview, Pete D'Alessandro (2018) talked about working in Waterloo in Black Hawk County during the general election campaigns of

2004, 2008, and 2016. Black Hawk County was one of six counties Clinton carried in 2016. While he was telling the story detailed below, he showed me a 2016 photo of the inside of the UAW Hall in Waterloo at noon on Election Day. In the picture, there were two phone canvassers working to mobilize Democrats.

Pete: In 2008, we worked out of the UAW Hall, the grassroots stuff that we were sending out. And what I remember was, out of both the office and the UAW Hall, we had this phone bank set up in the big room that they have there. And then we were actually doing canvas training in the parking lot because there were just so many people.

ADG: So, this was for Obama in '08?

Pete: This was for Obama in '08. So, it's not a Trump comparison necessarily, but, so think about what I just said. We have phone banks going like crazy for Obama in '08. And then we're literally moving the canvas training to outside because it was fairly decent weather and doing it out there so we're not getting in the way. This picture was taken at noon, in the same room, on Election Day in 2016.

ADG: In the UAW Hall?

Pete: In the UAW Hall.

ADG: Oh wow.

Pete: I purposely took that picture because that's when I texted someone and said, "I don't think we're going to do very well." And we won, so it had to be much worse other places. That's when it hit me that there was a different dynamic on our side of it, meaning the Democratic side, in terms of just the enthusiasm and the energy. ... and maybe there'll never be that kind of energy again. '08 obviously, the Barack Obama '12 campaign didn't have the energy of the '08 campaign. It was a unique, once in a generational thing maybe, but the point is that's a pretty telling picture. You know, at noon my phone bank is two people.

Second, Hillary Clinton's campaign events drew smaller crowds than Trump's did. A good number of Republican respondents discussed the size of Trump's rallies in the state. One Republican respondent from northeast Iowa, when asked to compare and contrast the grassroots operations of the two campaigns, compared the size of events for the two candidates:

"Trump was getting crowds of people to see and listen to him. The media would only show a small amount of the people who attended Clinton's talks making it look like there were big crowds of people who were there to cheer her on. Not a true picture." Another Republican respondent from southeast Iowa said, "Most of her campaign stops were in private settings and attracted very few people." According to Andy McGuire (2018), Iowa Democrats even had to "build crowds for Hillary," which was a change from previous cycles: "We never had to build crowds for Obama. Frankly, we haven't had to build crowds for, even back to Howard Dean."

Third, the lack of enthusiasm for Hillary Clinton was apparent to Iowa Democrats who participated in phone banks and canvassed door to door. Some respondents cited a lack of interest or even negativity when engaging prospective voters whom they believed were likely Clinton voters based upon previous elections. Respondents to the survey were asked an open-ended question about the presence of a moment during the campaign when they were convinced that Trump would win Iowa. Three answers to this item from Democratic respondents are particularly illustrative of the lack of enthusiasm that volunteers were experiencing while working for Clinton. One northeast Iowa Democrat believed Trump would win about one week prior to the election. While door knocking, the respondent indicated, "a lot of people didn't want to talk or just said they were not voting for Hillary." A northwest Iowa Democratic respondent said, "I don't think there was a moment, but more of a gradual realization. People were negative when I'd talk to them on the phone or door to door." Additionally, another northeast Iowa respondent had this to say about voter responses while door knocking:

> A good three months before the election when I was door-knocking, and at this time it was still mainly Democratic doors, I talked to a family that have been long-term Democrats. They told me they were all voting for Donald Trump because they just felt like we needed something different and that Hillary wasn't it. That whole day I heard the same story over and over again. Even from some good union people in town. I knew we had lost it. It was disheartening to do any of the work that needed to be done after that.

On the other side, enthusiasm for Donald Trump in Iowa was much higher. The enthusiasm for Trump was noted specifically in three of the four interviews with Republican political elites and mentioned in responses to several survey questions by both Democrats and Republicans. In describing Republicans, one northeast Iowa Democrat said, "Trump's supporters definitely had the wind to their backs since they worked with a message of shaking up things in Washington. There were a lot of excited Republicans who worked to get out his voters." Another northeast Iowa Democrat said, "Republicans seemed to be excited even though I know several of them weren't too excited about Trump being president, but they were hell-bent on not letting Clinton get in there. They were all over the place knocking on doors and having House parties and showing up to little town pubs and the like."

Some Republicans participants, both during interviews and participating in the survey, discussed the rapid growth of enthusiasm for Trump as a "movement." Eric Branstad (2018) said that he "saw and felt the movement" immediately after Trump won the nomination. In the lead up to Trump's first general election rally at the Adler Theatre in Davenport on July 28, 2016, every ticket for the event was spoken for two hours after the event was posted online. Governor Terry Branstad, Eric Branstad's father, and Senator Joni Ernst participated in the pre-program for the rally. Branstad characterized his experience at the rally in this way:

> My Dad got on stage and he didn't see what the crowd looked like but walking in everybody is on their feet. Adler Theatre filled with, I think 3,000 plus was the number, we were absolutely maxed out. Every seat, every like little rail filled, and my Dad got off the stage and said he "felt like a Beatle in the '60s." I mean everybody was on their feet, standing ovations, it was one of the most magical things he'd ever seen, I had seen, and I've grown up in this life and I've been in presidential politics, so really that was where the movement, for me, was really witnessed and got started.

Jeff Kaufmann (2019) indicated that Trump's rallies were nothing like he had ever seen. Kaufmann described a rally held later in the day on July 28 in Cedar Rapids as a "combination of a Baptist tent revival, an Amway convention, and a rock concert. To feel it was just, you just felt something." Trump continued to draw huge crowds at his rallies throughout the fall campaign; and juxtaposed against Clinton's smaller crowds, Trump's rallies revealed the growing enthusiasm gap in Iowa. In fact, when asked if there was a moment when a survey respondent knew Trump was going to win Iowa, a northeast Iowa Republican respondent said, "Any one of his rallies. The number of people that turned up, their enthusiasm."

The movement extended to Iowans who had not voted in years and even to Iowans who had never participated in politics. One southwest Iowa Republican respondent said, "President Trump gained many votes in our area from those who were either nonvoters in past elections or had voted for Obama in one term." A Democratic respondent from northeast Iowa described working the polls on Election Day in 2016 in this way:

> On Election Day, I poll watched and Republicans and No Party folks who I thought were dead because they never showed up to vote came with their walkers and canes determined to vote for Trump. … We are a red county … yet this county voted for President Obama in 2008 and in 2012 because the No Party voters supported him. The No Party people and even Democrats voted for Trump.

And it did not stop with vote switching. Several Republican respondents discussed having registered Democrats come to their headquarters to inquire about changing their party registration, offering to volunteer at party headquarters and even door knock, or they wanted to get a Trump yard sign. These passionate new volunteers were viewed as effective campaign "surrogates," particularly at the local level. Affectionately dubbed the "Trump Army" by Branstad (2018), they were willing to speak with friends, family, and neighbors about Trump and his candidacy. Branstad noted that these new volunteers were "fantastic on the phone" while working in Republican Party phone banks during the campaign, consistent with recent research which finds that local canvassers are more effective than non-local canvassers in driving voter turnout (Sinclair et al. 2013). Andy McGuire (2018) also recognized the unique role Trump supporters were playing in advocating for their candidate: "People who were for Trump wanted to tell 29 other people they were for Trump. They were evangelical about it and not in the religious sense, but they were spreading the word. They were disciples and so it felt like they had been deputized and they were supposed to help do this thing."

Also elevated out of the discussion on enthusiasm was the importance of Trump yard signs, "Make America Great Again" hats, and other promotional materials from the Trump campaign. Eric Branstad (2018) used the words "literally gold" when describing the paraphernalia coming from the national headquarters. Democratic and Republican county party officials began to understand the power of the movement once they saw Trump yard signs popping up all over the state. Andy McGuire (2018) noted that she saw Trump signs everywhere she went in the state. One Democratic respondent from northeast Iowa indicated that the signs served to "legitimize voting for him" because "you knew who your neighbors were supporting/voting for." Another Democratic respondent, also from northeast Iowa, said, "It became clear to me during the summer before the election when Trump signs sprouted up throughout my county like mushrooms, including at houses of previous Obama supporters. Trump's inevitable victory became even more obvious after the *Access Hollywood* video came out and not a single yard sign came down." Additionally, demand for Trump yard signs far exceeded the supply of signs coming from Trump's national headquarters. One southeast Iowa Republican respondent said the county party "could not keep signs in stock." Branstad described the demand for Trump yard signs in the following way: "As much as they would send us it would be out within two minutes. I would have my Allamakee County Chair drive all the way down [to the Des Moines metro] … to pick up 100-yard signs. That's all I would have to give them."

The shortage of Trump yard signs in the state created two opportunities in Iowa. First, it created an opportunity for the campaign to strategically distribute signs. Understanding the demand for the yard signs, the state campaign organization essentially converted the yard signs into a campaign currency of sorts. In his interview, Eric Branstad (2018) explained that process:

> Because they were such gold, I instructed my field staff, I said listen, in order to get a yard sign they need to make 90 calls at the phone bank or they need to go and knock on, I think it was 45 doors or 50 doors or something like that, and be a part of the volunteer team in order to take it, the yard sign. So, I could convert the yard signs into getting real voter touches.

Branstad went on to explain that the process described above was not a hard and fast rule. If a supporter came in for a sign and was not able to complete the canvassing tasks, Branstad instructed his field staff to "use good judgement" in deciding whether to give the supporter a yard sign. Second, the shortage of Trump yard signs also created an opportunity for enthusiastic Trump supporters to express their support by creating and displaying homemade yard signs. Branstad talked about the "countless stories" he heard of homemade yard signs popping up around the state. Branstad even shared a story about a picture he received from an Iowa farmer who had placed five round haybales together with Trump's name spelled out on them. The creation of handmade yard signs was yet another sign of the energy behind Trump's candidacy according to David Kochel (2018):

What you had were a lot of people putting, making their own yard signs and putting them up in their yards. I remember doing Joni Ernst's Roast and Ride in, gosh, it must have been June of 2016 before he was officially the nominee. And I remember riding through all of these towns kind of east of Des Moines seeing all these handmade yard signs up and I was thinking to myself that's when you know you've got a real amount of energy.

It is important to note that the Clinton campaign did not respond to the proliferation of mass-produced and homemade Trump yard signs. The Clinton campaign "decided they did not want to spend a lot of money on yard signs" (McGuire 2018). Not all Iowa Democrats agreed with the decision of the campaign, including Andy McGuire. She indicated that the campaign followed the old saying "yard signs don't vote." Two Democratic respondents to the survey disagreed with the approach. Both respondents, one from northeast Iowa and the other from southwest Iowa, argued that yard and field signs do matter in rural Iowa. McGuire believes that yard signs are an indication of voter support for a candidate and thus matter in Iowa elections. The result of the unwillingness by the Clinton campaign to spend money on yard signs was on full display as McGuire traveled the state:

I would go out and see people who had hand painted their barn with Trump. And nothing for us. Nothing. I mean, people made their own yard signs for us a little bit because they were so irritated by the whole thing, but we could have blanketed the place. They [Clinton's campaign] didn't think that was a good thing to do, but you could feel that the other side was literally putting their opinion out there for people.

2.3   Theme #2: Antipathy Toward Hillary Clinton

It was clear during the 2016 election cycle that neither Hillary Clinton nor Donald Trump was viewed very favorably by Americans. In fact, according to data from Gallup collected the week before the election, 42% of Americans viewed Trump "highly unfavorable" versus 39% for Clinton. According to Saad (2016), the ratings were "the worst election-eve images of any major-party presidential candidates" in Gallup's history. In Iowa during the week leading up to the election, however, Trump's unfavorability rating (50.7%), while still high, was more than 12 points better than Clinton's (62.9%) according to the Emerson College Poll (Kimball 2016).

Evidence of antipathy toward Hillary Clinton was also abundant in both the interview and survey responses. In referencing hatred or dislike of Clinton, some Republican respondents used the words "criminal," "crook," and "liar." Some referenced Clinton's time as Secretary of State and her involvement with the Benghazi attack and the Uranium One deal. Another Republican respondent cited the controversies surrounding the Clinton Foundation. In the interview with David Kochel (2018), Kochel said that Clinton "was not a good fit for Iowa." He noted a lack of comfort in campaigning in Iowa not only during the 2016 cycle but also dating back to the 2008 caucus campaign. Jeff Kaufmann (2019) probably best summed up the response of many Republican voters, particularly those who were skeptical of Trump at first: "I heard a lot of people saying we can't have Hillary. I think any analysis of this election, nationally or even at the macrolevel in Iowa, has to accompany the huge negatives Hillary had."

But antipathy toward Clinton was present among the responses of Democratic respondents as well. All respondents were asked an open-ended question regarding why Trump was able to flip 32 counties that Barack Obama won in 2012. Each respondent's answer was coded for up to five reasons why (i.e., "mentions"). The most frequent response to the question for both the first and second mentions referred to the rejection of Hillary Clinton as an explanation of the significant number of pivot counties in Iowa. It was also the leading explanation for Democratic respondents in the first and second mentions, but the leading explanation for Republican respondents for only the second mention. Additionally, when asked about why many Iowa non-partisans (i.e., "No Party" voters) voted for Trump in 2016 after supporting Obama in 2008 and 2012, the most frequent first mention in the recoded data was that non-partisans did not trust, like, or resonate with Hillary Clinton. When one Democratic party respondent from northeast Iowa was asked why Trump was able to flip 32 of the counties Obama won in 2012, one reason provided was "the overt hatred of Hillary Clinton—partly due to her gender but also due to possible Clinton fatigue. The Clintons have always been mired in controversy." Other Democratic respondents mentioned Clinton's use of a private email server while Secretary of State and how the fallout allowed Trump to drive the "Crooked Hillary" narrative. Another Democratic respondent from northwest Iowa, when asked to describe the 2016 general election, said, "Some long-time Democratic party loyalists I talked to didn't like or trust her." Finally, when asked if there was a moment from the 2016 campaign when he knew that Trump would win Iowa, Troy Price (2019) discussed a Clinton rally held in Ames the Saturday before the election. He said an individual, who had been vetted multiple times by the campaign, got up and said, "'Hillary Clinton is no different than Donald Trump. You should vote for Jill Stein.' All hell broke loose, and it was a terrible day. That was the day I realized we had lost Iowa. ... Thank God we're going to win it nationally, but it's not going to happen here. If this is what we are dealing with three days out, we're not going to win the state."

The genesis of the antipathy toward Clinton is not nearly as clear. A good number of Democratic respondents, and even a few Republican respondents, to the survey believe that the protracted, divisive primary campaign with Bernie Sanders was a major reason for the dislike or hatred of Hillary Clinton. In fact, when asked the question, "Do you believe that the lengthy primary campaign on the Democratic side played a role in shaping the outcome of the 2016 general election campaign here in Iowa," 45.5% of all respondents said it did. Another 9% of respondents said that it had a minimal impact on the outcome. Additionally, about a third of Democratic respondents to the survey knew of some effort by Sanders supporters to encourage other Sanders supporters to vote for anyone but Hillary Clinton.

Some Democratic respondents talked about the hard feelings some Sanders supporters felt after the caucuses because they felt cheated by the Iowa Democratic Party or the Democratic National Committee (i.e., they "stole the nomination"). In response, those Sanders supporters either voted for Jill Stein or Gary Johnson, or they stayed home altogether. Other Democratic respondents described the split as existing between younger Democratic voters and older Democratic voters. One Democratic respondent from northeast Iowa believed that inexperienced Sanders activists did not understand how nominations work, which led to attacks on Clinton and, ultimately, Trump's election:

> While I like and admire Bernie Sanders, I do believe his prolonged campaign had a negative effect. At the beginning, I thought it would be ok to have a little competition but as time wore on it became more anti-Clinton than an exercise in policy beliefs. The Bernie supporters were extremely focused on anti-Clinton and did not seem to care that dragging her down was eventually going to hurt the Democratic chances for President. Sanders stayed in too long and kept promising his supporters that if they kept up the fight

they would succeed. Often times the Bernie supporters were newbies who did not understand the complexities of nominating a presidential candidate. I know plenty of Bernie supporters who went to the Democratic convention thinking that they would change the eventual outcome of the nominee. Anyone with experience knew that by the time it gets to convention, the outcome is usually set. After Bernie failed to get the nomination, his supporters did not rally around Clinton and indeed I saw many things on Facebook etc. that continued to attack Hillary after the convention again not realizing they were really helping Trump and we got [what] we have now.

Others believe that, while the primary was indeed lengthy and divisive, it did not create the divide among the Democratic electorate in Iowa but simply exposed the divide. A northeast Iowa Democratic respondent argued that blaming Hillary's loss on the Sanders–Clinton primary is "scapegoating" and "wrong minded." What it boiled down to was "that there were a lot of people that just didn't like Hillary. And when she became the nominee the excited voters that were turned on by what Bernie was talking about just decided not to vote." The data collected from interviews also seems to suggest that the primary exposed—rather than created—the divide. Andy McGuire (2018) believes that the primary between Sanders and Clinton was not about issue differences but instead exposed a divide between Democrats who wanted an "experienced" candidate versus those who wanted a "newer, progressive" candidate. Jeff Link (2019) does not think the Democratic primary was a factor in deciding the outcome of the general election mainly due to Trump's nine point victory. However, it revealed a significant number of Democrats who would never support Clinton:

> I do think it was a problem for her. I don't know that it was related to Sanders. It could have been anybody in that spot. I think there was a plurality of Democrats who were not for Hillary Clinton no matter what for a variety of different reasons. Because she had been in the public eye and had been through so many battles for so long, you just sort of buildup scar tissue and I think that was a remnant of that.

Pete D'Alessandro (2018) agrees that the primary campaign was not a significant factor in the general election outcome. D'Alessandro has never "understood the concept of a candidate blaming voters because the voter didn't vote for them." He said the primary should have sent a "big red flag" to the Clinton campaign that should have triggered a reassessment to figure out how to win back Sanders voters in the general election. He believes the campaign never completed such a reassessment. Failing to complete such a reassessment could explain why Eric Branstad (2018) never saw any clear effort by the Clinton campaign to bring Sanders supporters back into the fold. It could also explain why Jeff Boeyink (2018) believes the campaign "had a hard time translating the enthusiasm" of Sanders supporters "to their ultimate nominee, Hillary Clinton."

2.4   Theme #3: Differences in Campaign Organization and Elite Support

Recruitment and mobilization of voters matter in political campaigns (Rosenstone and Hansen 1993; Verba et al. 1995). More recent research has focused on the impact of the "ground game" in American presidential elections to determine whether the ground game indeed matters. While some studies reveal significant effects that campaign field offices have on local media coverage (Darr 2019) and vote share (Masket 2009; Darr and Levendusky 2014), along with studies which focus on the effectiveness of canvassing efforts (e.g., Gerber and Green 2000; Middleton and Green 2008; Sinclair et al. 2013), the evidence supporting the importance of candidate appearances is mixed at best (e.g., Shaw 1999; King and Morehouse 2004; Holbrook and McClurg 2005; Chen and Reeves 2011; Wood 2016; Heersink and Peterson 2017; Devine 2018).

After Clinton's defeat, her campaign's ground game was blamed. Journalists wrote stories about her choice not to visit Wisconsin (Devine 2018). She did not have as many field offices in 2016 when compared to the number of field offices the Obama campaign had in 2012 (Darr 2017). More recently, however, there has been pushback on the idea that Clinton's ground game was to blame (e.g., Silver 2017; Devine 2018). During the 2016 campaign, journalists and scholars alike were questioning the ground game of the Trump campaign (e.g., Desjardins and Bush 2016; Masket and Victor 2016; Milligan 2016). It appeared different. Trump's campaign trailed the Clinton campaign in terms of field offices. Overall, it did not look like a traditional campaign organization. This epiphany is exactly what many political elites at the state and county level in Iowa observed about the two campaign organizations. On the Clinton side, they generally saw a more sophisticated, traditional establishment campaign. On the Trump side, they generally saw a non-traditional campaign organization. David Kochel (2018) described the two organizations using an analogy from Star Wars:

The Clinton campaign was kind of like the Imperial Death Star. It was well funded, well organized, but lacked passion. The Trump campaign was the scrappy rebels. They did not have a highly professional operation. They had staff and they, they made a lot of calls and did a lot of work, but ... it was not an organizational success. It was an electoral success and it was all based on message.

Clinton's campaign organization in Iowa was well-organized and staffed by experienced political operatives, indeed. Led by State Director Kane Miller and Senior Advisor Troy Price, the campaign had dedicated staff in the state for communications, digital operations, organizing, data analysis, voter protection, and get out the vote (Appleman 2017a). Estimates place the total number of staffers for Hillary for America in Iowa at around 40 paid staff.[6] As of mid-August 2016, the Iowa Democratic Party and the campaign had opened 24 field offices. The field offices were primarily located in central (6) and eastern Iowa (16). The campaign only had two field offices in western Iowa: One in Council Bluffs and one in Sioux City (Noble 2016a). Additionally, Clinton's staff in the state included political operatives who had experience not only working for Clinton during the primary phase, but also working for other candidates across the nation (Rynard 2016; Appleman 2017a). While many on Clinton's staff came to the state from other parts of the country, the staff also included native Iowans, individuals educated at one of Iowa's institutions of higher education, as well as those who had previously worked for Democratic candidates and elected officials in Iowa, such as former Senator Tom Harkin, former Governors Tom Vilsack and Chet Culver, and former Congressional candidate Monica Vernon.

Based upon the interview and survey data, the overall impression of the Clinton campaign by Iowa's political elites was mixed. Many agreed that the campaign organization was highly organized, professional, and had more resources and staff than the Trump campaign possessed. In fact, when asked to compare and contrast the two campaign organizations, Troy Price's (2019) initial response was, "We had one, they didn't." Several respondents to the survey had positive reflections on the effectiveness of the campaign. One northwest Iowa Democrat called it a "'normal' campaign based on issues and fact." Another central Iowa Democrat said it "was pretty decent. We saw increased Democrat voting, especially among our Hispanic community," which suggests that the strategic targeting of Hispanics may have mobilized voters in Iowa's communities with larger Hispanic populations.

Many survey respondents, however, were very critical of the campaign. In describing the Clinton campaign, multiple *Democratic* respondents compared it to the Obama ground game in 2008 and 2012. Those respondents believed Obama's was better. Another Democratic respondent used the words "good strategy" but "some flawed tactics." Four Democratic respondents from around the state, along with Jeff Link (2019), believed the campaign organization was too focused on the urban portions of the state, which may explain why three additional Democratic respondents from rural counties, in both northeast and northwest Iowa, said the campaign was not very visible within their counties. A northwest Iowa Republican respondent also mentioned this observation in a response to the question about campaign organizations, saying, "I saw very little Clinton ground game, again, part of that may be geography and knowing that they would be throwing money into a hole up here." This perception could be a function of the campaign deciding to locate its coordinated field offices in more urban locations in central and eastern Iowa. Additionally, it could be a function of the Clinton campaign knowing that they could not win Iowa early on (Kochel 2018). Two Democratic respondents from rural counties questioned whether the national campaign believed it could win Iowa as well; as a result, outreach to more rural parts of the state was not conducted: "As for the Clinton campaign, it felt that they abandoned Iowa pretty early in the campaign. There wasn't much of a Clinton presence in my county" (northeast Iowa Democratic respondent). Andy McGuire (2018) discussed this observation as well during her interview. She indicated that the national campaign pulled resources from the state a few weeks prior to the election because they no longer believed they could win the state, which required the Iowa Democratic Party to backfill funds for the last few statewide mailings from the coordinated campaign.

Finally, participants from both parties specifically criticized the Clinton campaign's approach to campaigning in Iowa. Several participants posited that the campaign was "overconfident" and took Iowa, and the entire upper Midwest, for granted. One Republican respondent from northwest Iowa said, "I think the Clinton campaign was expecting her to win in Iowa so they did not work as hard." Another Republican respondent from southeast Iowa said, "Clinton took a lot for granted" and "Trump did not take anything for granted." A southeast Iowa Democrat noted, "The attitude, Obama won in Iowa twice, certainly we will win again was prevalent." Troy Price (2019) also believes this to be true. He mentioned the national campaign assumed that Iowa and the upper Midwest "would just be there" in the Clinton column.

Other participants cited the campaign's hierarchical, "top-down" approach to running the campaign in the state. Jeff Kaufmann (2019) called the campaign "scripted," meaning that directives were coming from the national headquarters to be implemented at the state and local levels. Because the campaign was structured hierarchically, several local party leaders from northeast and southeast Iowa felt their input was not welcome. They did not perceive any "coordination with the locals" and that "a lot of strategic direction" was "coming from state-level organizers" with "very little communication being sent back up the chain from the local and regional organizers on the ground." One northeast Iowa Democratic respondent even went as far as to say that "Clinton was very top-down, and they knew better than the people on the ground."

One reason which may explain why Clinton's campaign was viewed so poorly by some (i.e., ignored rural Iowa and top-down approach) was its focus on data analytics to drive campaign strategy. In fact, Jeff Link (2019) indicated that analytics was *the* driver of the campaign: "They were very driven by analytics, and so if the analytics told them that they're better off working in a precinct in Polk County than they are working any precinct in Carroll County, they went 100% by analytics. Not by local knowledge, not by history, not by anything. It was 100% driven by analytics." The problem, according to Link, was that the Clinton campaign's focus on analytics to refine targeting models did not help them in developing a "message that moves people":

> What the Clinton campaign conflated, I believe, is they used analytics to do everything. They didn't separate, sort of, message delivery with targeting, or message development with targeting, or message emphasis. So, for instance, in a number of states, battleground states, they didn't do traditional telephone surveys. They only did analytics surveys. … We did this for Obama all the time, but we did both. In an analytics survey you might ask three questions, but you have a sample size of 10,000. In a traditional telephone survey, you have a sample size of 800 or 1,000 and you ask a 20 minute survey because you ask a bunch of different issues, and you ask traits, attributes, and all sorts of different things. All the analytics is trying to do is tweak their model, so they'll make 10,000 calls every week to figure out, they were building a score of 0 to 100, and a 100 meant you were certain to vote for Hillary and a 0 meant you were certain to vote for Trump. They were trying to improve the deciles. That's all they were trying to do so that they would have more accurate targeting. Well, that doesn't help you figure out how to talk to somebody in Carroll, or in Elkader, or anywhere else.

Link believes there were voters, particularly No Party voters or late deciding voters, "who were up for grabs" if they had been "given a message" that resonated with them. This fact might explain why three survey respondents, two Democrats from northeast Iowa and one Republican from southwest Iowa, focused specifically on message when asked about campaign organizations: (1) "The Clinton people seemed to stay in the bigger cities and the House Parties they held seemed to be in big donor's homes. There were a lot of things done that I felt made her seem even more out of touch with regular people"; (2) "The Clinton grassroots effort was very strong and organized, but I think it missed the generic white, middle class, working voter. The Clinton campaign seemed to focus on the various diverse 'groups' and missed the largest group of all in Iowa. I suspect they felt this group would be there for them without working it"; and (3) "Democrat grassroots worked hard. They didn't have a good message."

The Trump campaign organization in Iowa, however, was unorthodox and non-traditional. Jeff Link (2019) believes that the "Trump campaign re-wrote all the rule books." To begin with, the national campaign organization was not all that large. They had not raised a lot of money compared to other candidates during the primary. Unlike previous campaigns, and unlike the Clinton campaign in 2016, the Trump campaign outsourced its data and digital operations. One of the greatest assets of the Iowa organization was its director, Eric Branstad, who brought knowledge of the Republican Party and Iowa politics to the campaign. Link argues, however, that Branstad and his team maximized the limited resources they were presented: "I don't think they gave him a lot of tools to work with other than Trump's time. And so I think they did more with less than any presidential campaign in memory."

The campaign had only 17 staffers statewide, including Branstad (Appleman 2017b). Nine of the staffers were located at the campaign's headquarters in Urbandale, a suburb of Des Moines. The statewide organization had a strategic focus on communications, which led to the hiring of two communications staffers. They also had a staffer responsible for coordinating events in the state (Branstad 2018). This strategic focus on communications and events most likely explains why multiple respondents to the survey mentioned the importance of the rallies Trump held around the state; the important role of social media platforms such as Twitter, Facebook, and Instagram; and the important role the media played in transmitting messaging.

Eight of the staffers were regional field directors: Each responsible for several counties, which varied depending upon the region. Many field directors did not work in field offices established by the campaign but rather in county party offices, public libraries, or community centers in the region. In fact, the only campaign office established in the state was the campaign's headquarters in Urbandale, which was a joint Republican National Committee (RNC)/Trump headquarters. According to a Republican campaign official I spoke with, field directors were expected to recruit local volunteers and activists for canvassing efforts. Once canvassers were identified, the field directors trained them on a digital app developed by the RNC to coordinate canvassing efforts. As this official mentioned, all canvassing operations were coordinated through the app, which meant that data collected while canvassing was uploaded directly to the campaign's databases. Additionally, the strategy was to train canvassers on the app and then have canvassers train additional volunteers to participate in further canvassing efforts. While the process was time consuming, "The result was passionate Iowa Republicans who were better than some of our paid staff at door knocking and GOTV efforts."

The Trump campaign organization really did not start to take shape until late in the summer of 2016 (Branstad 2018). There was a significant amount of turnover from Trump's staff after the Iowa Caucuses, which required Branstad to hire staff starting in late July and early August 2016 (Rynard 2016). As a result, the campaign was highly reliant on other political groups to help undertake key campaign roles early on in the general election campaign. According the Jeff Kaufmann (2019), the campaign "got organized when they needed to, but there was some disorganization" leading to both the Republican Party of Iowa and the County Central Committees taking on significant responsibilities during the campaign. Resource sharing, within federal elections restrictions, was "unprecedented." Kaufmann also felt the "coordination of messaging" was high and the state party could help shape messaging. Kaufmann characterized it as unifying "the levels and layers of a campaign."

The RNC also stepped in to fill significant gaps in the state and around the country. Kaufmann (2019) indicated that they "came to the rescue" with their digital and grassroots operations. The RNC provided the "resource driven, the technology driven pieces that the campaign needed," which made a huge difference at the microlevel. Kaufmann discussed what he called the "transformation of Reince Preibus" during the cycle. Like other Iowa Republicans, Reince Preibus, the Chair of the RNC, was also quite skeptical of Trump's candidacy in the beginning. Kaufmann posits that his transformation from skeptic to supporter cannot be underestimated in understanding the role the RNC played in 2016: "Without Reince Preibus making the decision that he was all in and providing extraordinary amounts of resources to Donald Trump in places like Iowa, he may have won Iowa, but it wouldn't have been by almost 10%. The RNC came to the rescue in a major, major logistical way."

A number of advocacy groups formed to advocate on behalf of Trump as well (Appleman 2017b). When describing the Trump campaign organization, one Republican survey respondent from southwest Iowa said, "The grassroots operations for the Trump campaign developed from a loose-knit operation at first and transformed up through Election Day into one where Republican organizations found a common backing for Trump." What this response suggests is that the creation of the advocacy groups helped coalesce support around Trump's candidacy. Groups such as Iowa Women for Trump, Iowa Christian Conservatives for Trump, Iowa Veterans for Trump, Iowa Agriculture for Trump, and Pro-Life Iowans for Trump became integral parts of the grassroots network for the campaign, solidifying the support of key Republican constituencies that Trump needed to win the state.

If county party officials were looking for an extensive ground game from the Trump campaign, they were certainly disappointed. It was clear from the survey responses that county party officials were not seeing much of a ground game within their counties. Multiple respondents from both parties reported not seeing a significant ground game in their counties, using phrases like "no ground game," "no evidence of a grassroots campaign," "very little of it," and "non-existent" to describe the grassroots efforts they observed on behalf of the Trump campaign. One Republican respondent from southwest Iowa indicated that after the national convention in July, their "area did not see a great deal of campaign workers directly, but our local party organization did actively outwork the competition." Due to the unique nature of the candidate and the campaign, the lack of a strong ground game was probably not very important according to Jeff Boeyink (2018). Boeyink argues that "ground games cannot overcome what is going on organically with the voters." While ground games are important, Boeyink does not think Trump voters "were pushed by a ground game." They turned out as a result of the organic movement behind Trump's candidacy that was not going to be stopped.

It was mentioned previously that Hillary Clinton's message did not resonate, particularly with the "white, middle class, working voter." Donald Trump, however, did have the ability to connect, and his message resonated with "average" voters in 2016 according to several county party officials. One Republican respondent from southwest Iowa said, "Trump did remarkably well at connecting with people and his organization was able to solidify that feeling among voters." The "Make America Great Again" (MAGA) slogan was also identified as a powerful message for the Trump campaign, particularly for low information voters (McGuire 2018). One northeast Iowa Democratic respondent noted, "Make America Great Again was an excellent slogan. Since he never defined what that meant, each individual defined it for themselves. This created loyalty and translated to votes. Obama did the same thing with Hope and Change … it worked."

Finally, it is clear that "elite support" is closely related to organization and ground game. It has long been known that political elites, particularly partisan elites, can transmit important information to voters during elections (Miller and Shanks 1996). In the context of the 2016 election in Iowa, this phenomenon would take the form of endorsements from Iowa's elected officials. A trend that stood out in the interview data was the significant support that Iowa Republicans showed for Donald Trump. In multiple interviews, interviewees discussed the important role that Governor Terry Branstad; Lieutenant Governor Kim Reynolds; Senators Charles Grassley and Joni Ernst; and Representatives Rod Blum, David Young, and Steve King played in solidifying Republican support for Trump (Boeyink 2018; Branstad 2018; Kaufmann 2019; Link 2019). Jeff Kaufmann recalled Branstad, Reynolds, Ernst, and Blum standing with Trump at Joni's "Roast and Ride" in June 2016. He believed it sent a signal of "unity … to the rest of the state" and told Republicans who were hesitant to support him that it was okay to do so. Public support of Trump after campaign controversies, such as the release of the *Access Hollywood* tape, also sent a strong signal to Iowa Republicans that it was still acceptable to support Trump. Jeff Boeyink even credits Governor Branstad's early support of Trump after he secured the nomination, along with the backing of Jeff Kaufmann and the Republican Party of Iowa, for preventing a "Never Trump" movement from arising in the state.

There is also evidence in the survey which shows Governor Branstad's endorsement of Trump mattered to Trump voters in Iowa. Survey respondents were asked the following question regarding elite support: "How important were each of the following to *Trump* voters in your county? Gov. Branstad's Endorsement of Trump After Winning the Nomination." The answer choices ranged from "Not Important at All" (1) to "Extremely Important" (5). While the average score on the item was 3.48, which falls between "Moderately Important" and "Quite Important," 31.7% of respondents saw the endorsement as "Quite Important" and 16.7% of respondents saw it as "Extremely Important" to Trump voters. Republican respondents, with an average score of 3.62, were slightly more likely view the endorsement as important. Democratic respondents had an average score of 3.39 on the item. The difference, however, is not statistically significant ($t = -0.94$, $p = 0.348$).

On the Democratic side, elite support was hard to find. During the 2008 and 2012 presidential campaigns, the Obama campaign could expect elite support from the likes of former Senator Tom Harkin, former Governor Tom Vilsack, and former Representatives Leonard Boswell and Bruce Braley (McGuire 2018). In 2016, the most recognizable federal or statewide elected official on the Democratic side from Iowa was Representative Dave Loebsack.[7] This reality put Iowa Democrats in a bind because they no longer had the surrogates to go out and help with fundraising, voter turnout efforts, and messaging. Most importantly, Iowa Democrats who were hesitant to support Hillary Clinton did not have this critical "elite cue" from Democratic elected officials that it was alright to support the party's nominee.

2.5   THEME #4: THE RURAL–URBAN DIVIDE MATTERS SIGNIFICANTLY IN IOWA

Donald Trump's electoral strength in 2016 resided in rural counties all over the country (Gambio and Keating 2016). As presented in Chap. 1, Trump won every rural county in Iowa, only losing the popular vote in six major urban counties in central and eastern Iowa. Some may question how a billionaire from Manhattan could come into rural America and resonate with rural voters. Americans, however, should not be surprised that Trump's message resonated in rural America. Rural Americans, including many rural Iowans, feel disrespected by people who live in urban areas and ignored by government (Cramer 2016; Wuthnow 2018). They feel left behind in the new global economy, as jobs disappear and wages grow stagnant. Many in rural America yearn for the good old days because they believe that life oriented around farming was "simpler" and, quite frankly, better (Struthers and Bokemeier 2000, 42). Trump's appeal in rural America is grounded in this perception. Trump was the "change agent." Clinton was the "status quo." He was going to "Drain the Swamp." She was going to extend Obama's legacy. His focus was on jobs, stagnant wages, bad trade deals, and "Making America Great Again." Her focus was on protecting Obamacare, fighting for equal rights, and continuing to pursue free trade (Longworth 2016). Rural Americans wanted someone who would fight for them and the issues they cared about. They saw Trump as the answer.

The state political elites I interviewed and many of the respondents to the survey of county party officials recognized the importance of understanding the rural–urban divide in Iowa politics, not only in the context of the 2016 election but also in moving forward toward 2020 and beyond. All eight state political elites I interviewed demonstrated a great understanding of the divide itself and some of its underlying causes. They believed it had a significant impact on the 2016 race and will continue to create unique challenges in the future. Survey respondents were asked the question, "Do you believe the rural-urban divide in Iowa had an impact on the 2016 presidential election?" Two-thirds of all respondents said that it had. The additional qualitative data provided by participants outlines what they believe are the root causes of support for Donald Trump in rural Iowa, many of which mirror those in the preceding paragraph.

First, there is some evidence that rural voters feel ignored by government. In discussing her travels around the state, Andy McGuire (2018) noted that the differences are not based on issue positions. Her perception reveals that voters in rural Iowa care about the same issues as those in urban areas. The differences deal with how they perceive government and how they perceive being treated by government:

On the issues, they're the same. When you sit down and talk to them, their worries are exactly the same. It's stunningly the same. You can't figure out any difference. But they feel like they're not getting the good end of the stick. Their chip on their shoulder. ... They feel like their tax dollars go in and don't come back. They feel like nobody pays attention, none of the laws and rules are helping them. And they blame Democrats for that. And yet their issues are the same. ... We've gotta somehow make rural people realize we're listening. We are doing things just for you. The reality doesn't match what they think, but they think it and so that's what's important. I always tell people it doesn't matter what reality is, it matters what people think and people think that they're not getting the good end of the stick.

McGuire is puzzled as to how to solve the disconnect between perception and reality. She believes part of the problem includes the way rural Iowans view the two parties; in other words, Democrats "tend to represent urban" and Republicans "tend to represent rural." Another part of the problem is messaging, and McGuire asserted that if she could have figured out how to more effectively communicate with rural Iowans, "I would have done it."

Second, the economics of rural Iowa are different than in the urban areas of the state. While urban areas have felt the positive effects of recovery from the Great Recession, rural areas are still struggling to recover (Boeyink 2018). There is a "resentment" in rural Iowa "toward cities" and "toward politicians from cities" because rural Iowans themselves are "not a part of the innovation and growth that is taking place in cities" (Kochel 2018). Poverty is also a significant issue in rural Iowa, which certainly shapes political attitudes. One Democratic respondent from rural Iowa discussed the linkage between poverty and Trump's messaging in a response regarding the rural–urban divide in Iowa:

> Much poverty in rural Iowa. I ask the local schools for their Free and Reduced Lunch percentages to see if we are gaining or losing. We are losing big time. When I was on the school board, maybe 26%. Now in the mid to upper 40s. The MAGA slogan resonated. Tax cuts driving job creation.... more money in my paycheck and maybe a higher paying job. Win/win. They voted for their perceived self-interest. In the long run, it may be against their interest when the government services that they rely on are cut. (like free and reduced)

Coupled with the perception that government is not responsive, economic struggles in rural Iowa have led rural voters to feel left behind. The result is that rural voters will look to candidates who provide an economic message which resonates with them. As Troy Price (2019) put it, "People in rural Iowa already feel left behind. They already feel like their towns are falling apart, falling away ... We just didn't give them a message that made them feel like we would be with them. That we were fighting for them."

Message was a significant issue in the 2016 election, particularly when evaluating rural versus urban voters. Trump "paid attention and had a message that related to rural Iowa" (Link 2019). The "Make America Great Again" slogan from the Trump campaign resonated in rural Iowa. In the words of one northeast Iowa Democratic respondent, Trump made "big promises which made them feel good about a brighter future." It gave rural Iowans economic hope for the future in the form of economic renewal and "a promise of better wages" (northwest Iowa Democratic respondent). Ultimately, "Even though Donald Trump is a billionaire, I think they saw in him, whether you find it remarkable or not, they found somebody who actually was in touch with the plight of people facing those kinds of economic hardships" (Boeyink 2018).

Hillary Clinton, on the other hand, did not deliver a message which resonated with rural Iowa voters, and it was not seen as authentic in rural Iowa. One southeast Iowa Democrat said, "Many of the issues put forward by the Democrats did not resonate in rural areas. This is a highly conservative county" and the "big issues were abortion and gays." A Democratic respondent from northeast Iowa described the differences in issue importance between voters in rural versus urban areas: "Rural Iowan's continue to look for someone to save their communities, increase their wages, and provide better healthcare. Urban Iowan's didn't put as much weight into those issues when choosing a candidate." Several Democratic survey respondents from rural Iowa noted that Clinton's message not only failed to resonate in rural Iowa, but she outright ignored rural Iowa, even saying that her campaign "lacked in their outreach to rural Iowans." Not surprisingly, there were questions about whether Clinton even cared about rural Iowans. One northeast Iowa Democratic respondent went as far as to say "I do not think rural voters could relate to Hillary Clinton. She seemed out of touch and did not understand their way of life and challenges." Jeff Boeyink (2018) agreed, and in doing so, also argued that Clinton's "Basket of Deplorables" comment certainly did not help her win over rural Iowa voters. In his words, "The 'Basket of Deplorables' was a devastating hit to her in places like Lee County or Keokuk County … I think they saw an out of touch elitist in Hillary Clinton." Respondents to the survey also believed the "Basket of Deplorables" comment was an important factor for Trump voters. Respondents were asked to rate the importance of the comment to Trump voters. 37.3% of respondents rated it "Quite Important" and 49.2% rated it "Extremely Important." The average score on the item was 4.27, which falls between the two highest ratings of importance.

2.6   Theme #5: 2016 Was a "Change" Election

Political scientists have long known that many voters assess presidential candidates "retrospectively," or backward-looking (Key 1966; Fiorina 1981). In doing so, voters use information such as personal financial condition or perceptions about the national economy to assess the performance of the president. If the president is viewed favorably, then voters will reward the incumbent with another term. If the president is viewed unfavorably, then voters will vote to make a change. This vetting can also be used to assess a candidate from the incumbent's party who is running when the incumbent is termed out. In the case of the 2016 presidential election, exit polling data seems to suggest that retrospective evaluations were important to many voters. According to exit polls (Exit Polls 2016a, b), voters who viewed the national economy as "poor" supported Trump 62%-31%. In Iowa, the gap was even wider: 71%-22%. Voters who believed their personal financial condition was "worse" favored Trump 77%-19%. Trump's support in Iowa was 5% higher (82%) for those who felt worse off financially. For those who disapproved of President Obama's performance, nearly 90% of voters supported Trump both nationally and in Iowa. Voters who indicated they were "angry" at the federal government were nearly four times as likely to vote for Trump as they were for Clinton (75%-18%). In Iowa, they were between seven to eight times more likely (81%-11%). Finally, 39% of all Americans and 43% of Iowans believed that the most important candidate quality was a candidate who could "bring change." For those voters, 82% voted for Trump nationally and 87% voted for Trump in Iowa.

Respondents to the survey also indicated that change or retrospective evaluations were important to Iowa voters. When asked about dynamics within the 32 pivot counties in Iowa, multiple respondents offered answers which were oriented toward disappointment in the Obama administration, the belief that Donald Trump would help solve problems, and the desire for something new. These types of responses were seen in the first, second, and third mentions, which were recoded as described previously. Evidence of "change voting" was also present in the open-ended responses to the question "Why the shift in candidate preference by Iowa non-partisans?" Once again, numerous respondents said that the shift was due to Trump being an outsider, that Trump cared about them and issues important to them, that voters wanted something new, and that the establishment had left them behind.[8]

Two elements of "change voting" emerged from the qualitative data. First, 2016 was viewed by many as a referendum on President Obama's performance. Many voters were looking for a change because they had yet to feel the economic recovery after the recession; in a lot of rural communities, they were still "slowly bleeding and hurting" (Price 2019). A central Iowa Democratic respondent discussed how economic disadvantage played a role in rural Iowa as well:

> When I spoke to constituents at their doors, people literally had roofs caving in on their homes, severe medical issues, and stagnant wages. So many people told me they had voted for Obama, and he didn't help them, so they were going to vote for Trump. No matter how many different ways I tried to explain that Obama had a broken congress and that the tea-party "liberty" party continued to block legislation, the message didn't get through to them.

These voters were looking for something different in 2016, as many of them had in 2008 and 2012 when they supported Obama. This fact is especially true for many No Party voters who were vote switchers in 2016 (Boeyink 2018; Link 2019). Many No Party voters were "let down by the Democrats," who they entrusted to fix problems in Washington, particularly economic problems like jobs and wages. Vote switchers "didn't see the results that they were hoping to see with the previous administration" (Branstad 2018). So why Trump? They thought he could fix the problems the establishment had not been able to fix because he was "the antithesis of Hillary Clinton, and in a lot of ways, Barack Obama. ... People just felt like it was time to shake things up" (Price 2019).

Second, 2016 was a rejection of politics as usual in Washington, D.C. During his interview, Jeff Kaufmann (2019) discussed the "strain of populism," or "the middle finger at the establishment," that is prevalent in the Iowa electorate, particularly in rural areas. Kaufmann argues we saw it in the primary season between Bernie Sanders and Hillary Clinton, as well as between Donald Trump and "the Bush folks." Then, during the general election, there were a significant number of voters "who were going to vote for a populist no matter what" (D'Alessandro 2018). When evaluating the interview and survey data, evidence of populism was present. In the words of Jeff Boeyink (2018), the 2016 election was a "stark repudiation of business as usual in Washington." When asked to describe the 2016 election, a Republican survey respondent from northeast Iowa said it was "an election where the disenchanted electorate that was frustrated with the process came back to the process because they found a champion of their cause in Donald Trump," suggesting that voters frustrated with "business as usual" were willing to participate again, or possibly for the first time, because they had found their "change agent." David Kochel (2018) also discussed how Trump used his status as an "outsider" candidate to attract not only Republican voters but also No Party voters. Many No Party voters "bought into his message of being an outsider," which was anti-Washington and anti-politics. They believed Trump would go to Washington and "knock some heads," to "knock the crap out of Washington." This image was appealing to them because the establishment had been unable to solve their problems, so maybe a billionaire businessman from outside of the establishment could.

2.7 Conclusion

The themes identified from the original dataset of qualitative interview and survey data paint an interesting picture of the 2016 presidential election in Iowa. The data portray a large enthusiasm gap between candidates Donald Trump and Hillary Clinton, no doubt driven in part by the significant amount of antipathy toward Clinton which dates back to the 2008 campaign cycle if not earlier. The data also reveals significant differences in terms of how participants viewed the two political campaigns. Clinton's campaign was viewed as very traditional, focused on building a network of experienced political operatives, and driven by analytics. Trump's organization, however, was viewed as very non-traditional and minimal. It was very grassroots-driven and was fueled by Trump supporters all over the state, who were willing to volunteer their time to work as canvassers or were willing to speak with friends, family, and neighbors about their support for Trump. The data also explains why understanding the rural–urban divide in the state is so important as attitudes, along with economic and political characteristics, differ so significantly between the urban and rural areas of Iowa. Additionally, it demonstrated there was a perception that Hillary Clinton was not visible enough in rural Iowa, essentially ceding rural Iowa to Trump. Finally, the data identifies that populism was an important factor in shaping vote choice in Iowa during 2016, especially for No Party voters and for voters who switched course in 2016 after supporting Barack Obama in 2008 or 2012.

Some political scientists and observers of Iowa politics may be reading this chapter wondering about the role of sexism or racial attitudes during the 2016 campaign. Was the antipathy toward Hillary Clinton driven by predispositions toward traditional gender roles? Was support for Donald Trump driven by racial attitudes cued by his rhetoric regarding Hispanic immigrants or Muslims? There are certainly theoretical reasons to believe that sexism and racism could have played a role, and it is certainly plausible sexism or racism played a significant role in shaping attitudes about Hillary Clinton or shaping vote choice for Donald Trump. However, sexism and racism are not identified as major themes in this chapter primarily because the evidence for them is mixed at best.

As discussed in the methods section above, the first nine or ten questions in the survey were open-ended questions which were mirrored in the interview schedule. While some focused on specific issues and made it possible that respondents would have not discussed sexism or racism as a result, other questions were much more open-ended, topically. It is safe to assume that if sexism and racism were indeed perceived to be significant factors in shaping the outcome in 2016, then a significant number of respondents and interviewees would have identified these concepts in other open-ended questions. The reality is that sexism and racism were only mentioned a handful of times in survey responses, but they did not show up in the interview data until after a specific question about sexism and racism (Question 6) was asked. In fact, outside of Questions 3 and 5 on the survey, sexism and racism were only mentioned three times each. For Question 3 regarding pivot counties, sexism was mentioned in three different responses and racism was mentioned in five. For Question 5 regarding vote switching by No Party voters, sexism was mentioned in five different responses and racism in three.

Question 6 on the survey and in the interview schedule specifically asked participants "Do you believe that racist or sexist attitudes significantly factored into the voting calculus of Iowa voters?" In the survey data, about half of all respondents (48.5%) believed racism was a factor and 46.8% of all respondents believed sexism was a factor. Most respondents who believed racism and sexism were a factor were Democratic respondents (31 of 32 for racism and 29 of 29 for sexism). Ten Democratic respondents believed racism was not an issue, and eight Democratic respondents did not believe sexism was an issue in 2016. Common responses for Republican respondents, rebutting the influence of racism and sexism included reference to Barack Obama winning the state in 2008 and 2012[9] as well as the election of Senator Joni Ernst in 2014 and Governor Kim Reynolds in 2018. In the interview data collected after asking Question 6, the results were mixed again. Two interviewees ruled both ideas out immediately and one argued that racism played a role due to Trump's rhetoric on immigration. The remaining five interviewees were somewhere in between, with the prevailing attitude being that racism or sexism may have played a role in 2016, but the role they played was minimal and not alone determinative. Several Democratic respondents to the survey also believed that racism or sexism played a minimal yet not significant role.

As we turn to Chaps. 3 and 4, quantitative models of vote choice will be developed using county-level and individual-level data to more fully explain support for Donald Trump in Iowa during the 2016 election. The role of racial attitudes will be examined in both chapters to more fully resolve the question of whether racial attitudes factored into the decisions of Iowa voters.[10]

Notes

1. The survey questionnaire and interview schedule are available from the author upon request. Data collection for the survey of county party officials and interviews of state political elites was cleared by the Central College Institutional Research Board on November 13, 2018 (IRB #H-45-F2018-AG).
2. The reports are housed in a database by the Iowa Ethics & Campaign Disclosure Board: https://webapp.iecdb.iowa.gov/PublicView/?d=county.
3. The pre-survey letter and survey process began in mid-November to avoid overlap with the 2018 midterm election. If the survey had been distributed during the campaign, it was feared that county party officials may have ignored the invitation.
4. Geographic region boundaries were based upon the Iowa Department of Transportation's 511 Social Media Sites (https://iowadot.gov/511/511-social-media-sites). The NE/NW overlapped counties were reallocated with Hamilton, Hancock, Winnebago, and Wright Counties in northwest Iowa and Butler, Floyd, Grundy, and Mitchell Counties in northeast Iowa.
5. In transcribing specific quotes from the interview recordings, filler phrases such as "ums," "uhs," "ands," or "you know" have been filtered out.
6. This does not include staff from the Iowa Democratic Party who were working with the campaign to elect Clinton. Including coordinated campaign staff would increase the number to between 150 and 200 staffers in Iowa.
7. McGuire notes the lack of elite support was not due to an unwillingness to support Clinton, but an inability to be on the campaign trail during 2016. Boswell was defeated in 2012, no longer in Congress, and fighting cancer. Braley gave up his House seat in 2014 to run for the Senate and was defeated by Joni Ernst. After the election, he moved to Colorado. Neither Harkin nor Vilsack could undertake partisan advocacy during 2016. Harkin

had retired from the Senate in 2014 and was working on his nonpartisan institute at Drake University in Des Moines. Vilsack was still serving in the Obama administration as the Secretary of Agriculture. This left Loebsack as the only federal elected official on the Democratic side.

8. Question 5 of the survey was recoded following the same process used to recode Question 3. Please see Sect. 2.3 for a detailed description.

9. There are theoretical reasons in the literature which explain why Obama voters could shift their votes to Trump in 2016 based upon racial bias. For example, see Sides et al. (2018).

10. Unfortunately, no measure of sexism is available in an individual-level dataset of 2016 Iowa voters. See note 1 in Chap. 4 for more information regarding why the role of sexism in explaining 2016 vote choice is not investigated further using survey data.

REFERENCES

Appleman, Eric M. 2017a. Clinton 2016 General Election Campaign Organization, Iowa. Last Modified July 21, 2017. http://www.p2016.org/clinton/clinton-genia.html.

———. 2017b. Trump 2016 General Election Campaign Organization, Iowa. Last Modified on May 26, 2017. http://www.p2016.org/trump/trump-genia.html.

Boeyink, Jeff. 2018. Interview by Author. *Des Moines*, December 17.

Branstad, Eric. 2018. Interview by Author. *Des Moines*, December 13.

Chen, Lanhee J., and Andrew Reeves. 2011. Turning Out the Base or Appealing to the Periphery? An Analysis of County-Level Candidate Appearances in the 2008 Presidential Campaign. *American Politics Research* 39 (3): 534–556. https://doi.org/10.1177%2F1532673X10385286.

Cramer, Katherine J. 2016. *The Politics of Resentment: Rural Consciousness in Wisconsin and the Rise of Scott Walker*. Chicago: University of Chicago Press.

D'Alessandro, Pete. 2018. Interview by Author. *Des Moines*, December 19.

Darr, Joshua. 2017. The Incredible Shrinking Democratic Ground Game. *Mischiefs of Faction*, November 16. https://www.vox.com/mischiefs-of-faction/2017/11/16/16665756/shrinking-democratic-ground-game.

———. 2019. Earning Iowa: Local Newspapers and the Invisible Primary. *Social Science Quarterly* 100 (1): 320–327. https://doi.org/10.1111/ssqu.12565.

Darr, Joshua P., and Matthew S. Levendusky. 2014. Relying on the Ground Game: The Placement and Effect of Campaign Field Offices. *American Politics Research* 42 (3): 529–548. https://doi.org/10.1177%2F1532673X13500520.

Desjardins, Lisa, and Daniel Bush. 2016. The Trump Campaign Has a Ground-Game Problem. *PBS News Hour*, August 30. https://www.pbs.org/newshour/politics/trump-campaign-has-ground-game-problem.

Devine, Christopher J. 2018. What If Hillary Clinton *Had* Gone to Wisconsin? Presidential Campaign Visits and Vote Choice in the 2016 Election. *The Forum* 16 (2): 211–234. https://doi.org/10.1515/for-2018-0011.

Exit Polls. 2016a. Exit Polls: National President. Last Modified November 23, 2016. https://www.cnn.com/election/2016/results/exit-polls.

———. 2016b. Exit Polls: Iowa President. Last Modified November 23, 2016. https://www.cnn.com/election/2016/results/exit-polls/iowa/president.

Fiorina, Morris P. 1981. *Retrospective Voting in American National Elections.* New Haven, CT: Yale University Press.

Gambio, Lazaro, and Dan Keating. 2016. How Trump Redrew the Electoral Map, from Sea to Shining Sea. *Washington Post.* Last Modified November 9, 2016. https://www.washingtonpost.com/graphics/politics/2016-election/election-results-from-coast-to-coast/.

Gerber, Alan S., and Donald P. Green. 2000. The Effects of Canvassing, Telephone Calls, and Direct Mail on Voter Turnout: A Field Experiment. *American Journal of Political Science* 94 (3): 653–663. https://doi.org/10.2307/2585837.

Heersink, Boris, and Brenton D. Peterson. 2017. Truman Defeats Dewey: The Effect of Campaign Visits on Election Outcomes. *Electoral Studies* 49: 49–64. https://doi.org/10.1016/j.electstud.2017.07.007.

Holbrook, Thomas M., and Scott D. McClurg. 2005. The Mobilization of Core Supporters: Campaigns, Turnout, and Electoral Composition in United States Presidential Elections. *American Journal of Political Science* 49 (4): 689–703. https://doi.org/10.1111/j.1540-5907.2005.00149.x.

Kaufmann, Jeff. 2019. Interview by Author. *Des Moines,* February 14.

Key, V.O. 1966. *The Responsible Electorate: Rationality in Presidential Voting, 1936–1960.* Cambridge, MA: Harvard University Press.

Kimball, Spencer. 2016. Emerson College Poll: Iowa Leaning for Trump 44% to 41%. Grassley, Coasting to a Blowout, Likely to Retain Senate Seat. *Emerson College Poll,* November 4. https://www.scribd.com/document/330116136/11-4-Iowa-Emerson.

King, David C., and David Morehouse. 2004. Moving Voters in the 2000 Presidential Campaign: Local Visits, Local Media. In *Lights, Camera, Campaign! Media, Politics, and Political Advertising,* ed. David A. Schultz, 301–317. New York: Peter Lang Publishing.

Kochel, David. 2018. Interview by Author. Phone. December 18, 2018.

Langer, Gary. 2016. Clinton, Trump All But Tied as Enthusiasm Dips for Democratic Candidate. *ABC News,* November 1. https://abcnews.go.com/Politics/clinton-trump-tied-democratic-enthusiasm-dips/story?id=43199459.

Link, Jeff. 2019. Interview by Author. *Des Moines,* January 3.

Longworth, Richard C. 2016. Disaffected Rust Belt Voters Embraced Trump. They Had No Other Hope. *The Guardian,* November 21. https://www.theguardian.com/commentisfree/2016/nov/21/disaffected-rust-belt-voters-embraced-donald-trump-midwestern-obama.

Masket, Seth E. 2009. Did Obama's Ground Game Matter? The Influence of Local Field Offices During the 2008 Presidential Election. *Public Opinion Quarterly* 73 (5): 1023–1039. https://doi.org/10.1093/poq/nfp077.

Masket, Seth, and Jennifer Victor. 2016. Clinton Has More Than 3 Times as Many Campaign Offices as Trump. How Much of an Advantage Is This? *Mischiefs of Faction*, October 5. https://www.vox.com/mischiefs-of-faction/2016/10/5/13174624/trump-field-offices.

McGuire, Andy. 2018. Interview by Author. *Des Moines*, December 18.

Middleton, Joel A., and Donald P. Green. 2008. Do Community-Based Voter Mobilization Campaigns Work Even in Battleground States? Evaluating the Effectiveness of MoveOn's 2004 Outreach Campaign. *Quarterly Journal of Political Science* 3 (1): 63–82. https://doi.org/10.1561/100.00007019.

Miller, Warren E., and J. Merrill Shanks. 1996. *The New American Voter*. Cambridge, MA: Harvard University Press.

Milligan, Susan. 2016. The Fight on the Ground. *The Civic Report, U.S. News & World Report*, October 14. https://www.usnews.com/news/the-report/articles/2016-10-14/donald-trump-abandons-the-ground-game.

Noble, Jason. 2016a. Iowa Dems Announce 7 New Offices, Now Have 24 Statewide. *Des Moines Register*, August 17. ProQuest.

———. 2016b. Early Voting Numbers in Iowa Revealed. *Des Moines Register*, October 22. ProQuest.

Price, Troy. 2019. Interview by Author. Pella, IA. February 22.

Rosenstone, Steven J., and John Mark Hansen. 1993. *Mobilization, Participation, and Democracy in America*. New York: Macmillan Publishing.

Rynard, Pat. 2016. Clinton and Democrats Build an Army in Iowa for November. *Iowa Starting Line* (blog), July 19. https://iowastartingline.com/2016/07/19/clinton-and-democrats-build-an-army-in-iowa-for-november/.

Saad, Lydia. 2016. Trump and Clinton Finish with Historically Poor Images. *Gallup News*, November 8. https://news.gallup.com/poll/197231/trump-clinton-finish-historically-poor-images.aspx.

Shaw, Daron R. 1999. The Effect of TV Ads and Candidate Appearances on Statewide Presidential Votes, 1988–96. *American Political Science Review* 93 (2): 345–361. https://doi.org/10.2307/2585400.

Shepard, Steven. 2015. The 2016 Enthusiasm Gap. *Politico*, December 30. https://www.politico.com/story/2015/12/2016-enthusiasm-republicans-democrats-217198.

Sides, John, Michael Tesler, and Lynn Vavreck. 2018. *Identity Crisis: The 2016 Presidential Campaign and the Battle for the Meaning of America*. Princeton, NJ: Princeton University Press.

Silver, Nate. 2017. Clinton's Ground Game Didn't Cost Her the Election. *FiveThirtyEight.com*, February 13. https://fivethirtyeight.com/features/clintons-ground-game-didnt-cost-her-the-election/.

Sinclair, Betsy, Margaret McConnell, and Melissa R. Michelson. 2013. Local Canvassing: The Efficacy of Grassroots Voter Mobilization. *Political Communication* 30 (1): 42–57. https://doi.org/10.1080/10584609.2012.737413.

Struthers, Cynthia B., and Janet L. Bokemeier. 2000. Myths and Realities of Raising Children and Creating Family Life in a Rural County. *Journal of Family Issues* 21 (1): 17–46. https://doi.org/10.1177%2F019251300021001002.

Verba, Sidney, Kay Lehman Schlozman, and Henry E. Brady. 1995. *Voice and Equality: Civic Voluntarism in American Politics*. Cambridge, MA: Harvard University Press.

Wood, Thomas. 2016. What the Heck Are We Doing in Ottumwa, Anyway? Presidential Candidate Visits and Their Political Consequence. *Annals of the American Academy of Political and Social Science* 667 (1): 110–125. https://doi.org/10.1177%2F0002716216661488.

Wuthnow, Robert. 2018. *The Left Behind: Decline and Rage in Rural America*. Princeton, NJ: Princeton University Press.

CHAPTER 3

Building a Winning Coalition: Understanding County-Level Support for Donald Trump in the 2016 Election

The big divide was that the Clinton campaign didn't really show up in rural Iowa, didn't have a message for rural Iowa, and basically let Trump do whatever he wanted in that area. Trump didn't really have a ground game that could take advantage of that, but he did have a message that resonated. He had some specific issues that he promised to work on and change and do things differently if he were elected. And Hillary didn't offer her version of that to those same voters.
—Jeff Link, *Iowa Democratic Strategist*

Abstract In this chapter, I present a discussion of the academic literature oriented toward presidential elections, Iowa elections, and the 2016 election. The literature is used to theoretically develop models of vote choice using county-level data. The county-level modeling reveals that Trump was able to build a winning coalition between core constituencies of the Republican base (i.e., Republican and evangelical voters), and secure the votes of white, working-class voters across the state. County-level models also indicate that Trump's improved performance over Mitt Romney in 2012 was driven by white, working-class voters as well, not by the core constituencies of the Republican base.

Keywords Republican • Evangelical • White, working-class voters • County

© The Author(s) 2020
A. D. Green, *From the Iowa Caucuses to the White House*,
Palgrave Studies in US Elections,
https://doi.org/10.1007/978-3-030-22499-8_3

93. This number is significant because it is the number of Iowa counties Donald Trump won in the 2016 presidential election. Trump won every county in western Iowa. Except for Polk and Story, he won every county in central Iowa. And outside of Black Hawk, Johnson, Linn, and Scott, he ran the table in eastern Iowa as well. He was the first Republican presidential nominee to win Des Moines and Wapello Counties in southeast Iowa since Richard Nixon in 1972 and the first to win Dubuque County in northeast Iowa since Dwight Eisenhower in 1956. All in all, Trump was successful in every corner of the state, outperforming Mitt Romney and pivoting 32 counties Barack Obama had won just four years prior (see Figs. 1.2 and 1.3 in Chap. 1).

As discussed in the previous chapter and the epigraph above, Trump's message was designed to assemble the winning coalition of voters necessary to win Iowa's six Electoral College votes and, ultimately, the presidency. He courted white, working-class voters in rural counties with a message of a new economic renaissance. Job creation. Wage growth. The end of terrible trade deals. He promised rural workers, who felt left behind by the pressures of globalization and urbanization, a renewed sense of hope for the future. At the same time, Trump needed to ensure that establishment Republicans and evangelical Christians, core constituents of the Republican base, stayed on board as well. He did so with a message of cutting taxes and regulations, along with a promise to appoint conservative judges to the Supreme Court. On Election Day, the question became whether the coalition would hold. Polling data in the last week of the campaign looked favorable for a Trump victory in Iowa. After the polls closed, the margins in many rural counties, particularly in eastern Iowa, exceeded expectations. While talking about eastern Iowa counties that had not been won by a Republican presidential candidate in nearly a generation, Eric Branstad (2018) said, "If I would have said the day before the election that we were going to win … with the margins that we did, they would have called me crazy."

At the national level, Trump was also able to successfully court white, working-class voters while still maintaining the core Republican constituency. He did well with evangelical voters, regular churchgoers, veterans, and rural voters (Byler 2017; Ceasar et al. 2017). A Q-analysis of Trump voters in 2016 by Rhoads et al. (2017) also identified many of these core Trump constituencies in the four factors of the analysis. Trump also benefitted from what Ceasar et al. (2017, 121) call "a flawed strategy" by the Clinton campaign, "which took for granted the Rust Belt, counted on reassembling the Obama coalition in full, and positioned her as a status-quo candidate in a change year." Clinton dominated in major urban areas around the country, but she also made inroads with white, college-educated voters in some suburban areas. She was hurt nationally, however, by the distribution of Hispanic and African American voters, a core constituency she needed to win, who primarily reside in non-Battleground states (Byler 2017; Silver 2017a).

The focus of Chap. 3 lies in explaining the support for Donald Trump at the county level in Iowa. In doing so, several questions are evaluated. First, was the "education gap" visible in the 2016 election in Iowa? Second, were the predictors associated with core Republican constituencies also powerful predictors of vote choice in 2016? Third, do economic variables, such as growth in median household income or changes in manufacturing employment within a county, help explain county-level election outcomes? Finally, are there significant differences in Trump support within rural versus urban counties? The models presented below document the importance of partisanship and the education gap in explaining support for Trump at the county level. Furthermore, it matters whether the county is rural or urban. However, evidence regarding the importance of county-level economic characteristics in explaining county-level support is mixed at best.

While the sheer number of counties in Iowa presents administrative and political challenges for government, it is ideal for researchers interested in analyzing county-level outcomes. To draw generalizations regarding county-level support for Donald Trump in 2016, seven predictors of Trump support were identified, and data was collected from a variety of sources to assess the importance of each indicator in predicting Trump's share of the two-party vote, Trump's overperformance of Mitt Romney in 2012, and the likelihood of the county being a pivot county in 2016. Before turning to the modeling, the theoretical linkage between the predictor and county-level support for Trump is developed based upon research in the field. A description of the data source for each predictor is provided as well.

3.1   Partisanship

Party identification has played a significant role in understanding voting behavior since the publication of *The American Voter* by Campbell et al. 1960 (Campbell et al.). *The American Voter* posits a model in which party identification is developed over time, beginning with socialization experiences early in life. Party ID is a long-term attitudinal predisposition, which then, in the context of elections, shapes the way voters perceive candidates, their campaigns, and the political information transmitted by candidates or the parties to voters. Party ID, according to Miller and Shanks (1996), is the "most enduring of political attitudes," built upon a "sense of individual attachment" to the party, not necessarily "formal membership in or active connection with a party organization" (117, 120). Partisans look to party leaders for information and cues in elections while simultaneously making decisions regarding candidates and issues. As Miller and Shanks (122) argue, "As new issues arise, and as new social problems develop, leaders must determine, help define, and then prescribe the appropriate beliefs and behaviors for the party." In the case of 2016, this acknowledgment may extend to elites in the Republican Party, who vouched for outsider Donald Trump after he won the Republican nomination.

Evidence of the strong relationship between party identification and vote choice dates back to *The American Voter* and is abundant across the political science literature. Generally speaking, partisans are much more likely to vote for their party's candidate, unless some short-term campaign force leads them to defect. In more recent years, voters in the electorate are much more partisan in their evaluation of candidates, particularly candidates of the opposing political party. Called "affective partisanship" or "negative partisanship," voters today are much more likely to view members of the other party negatively and members of their own party positively (Iyengar and Westwood 2015; Abramowitz and Webster 2016). This practice has consequences for voting behavior as it "has led to a sharp increase in party loyalty in voting for elected offices at all levels" and, ultimately, "a growing connection between the results of presidential elections and the results of House, Senate, and even state legislative elections" (Abramowitz and Webster 2016, 12). Abramowitz and McCoy (2019) also found evidence of negative partisanship during the 2016 cycle while examining the differences in the favorability scores for both Clinton and Trump.

There is significant evidence suggesting partisanship mattered during the 2016 election in Iowa. According to exit polls, the electorate that turned out on Election Day was split roughly in thirds: 31% Democratic, 34% Republican, and 35% Independent (Exit Polls 2016b). Ninety percent of Iowa Republicans stayed loyal and voted for Trump, while 88% of

Democrats voted for Clinton. Independents, or "No Party" voters, broke to Trump by a margin of 13% (51%-38%). Even though Trump won Iowa men 61%-33% and Clinton won Iowa women 51%-44%, the relationship between gender and vote choice was shaped by party ID. Clinton won both Democratic men (85%-13%) and women (90%-7%), while Trump won Republican men (92%-5%) and women (88%-7%). The two candidates split Independent voters, with Clinton winning Independent women 50%-42% and Trump winning Independent men 61%-26%. Furthermore, Iowa's Republican elite, including Governor Terry Branstad; Lieutenant Governor Kim Reynolds; Republican Party of Iowa Chairman Jeff Kaufmann; and Senators Charles Grassley and Joni Ernst, all endorsed Trump after he won the Republican nomination and stayed with him, even after his campaign was rocked by the release of the *Access Hollywood* tape in October 2016 (Hohmann 2016; Noble 2016a, b, c; Petroski 2016a, b). As discussed in Chap. 2, this elite support sent a cue to Iowa Republicans that it was still okay to support Donald Trump, baggage and all.

To assess the role partisanship played in explaining county-level support for Trump, the Republican share of total active voters in each county as of November 1, 2016, was included in the modeling (IA SOS 2016b). It is expected that the share of active Republican voters is positively related to support for Trump, meaning counties with a higher share of active Republican voters should have a higher share of the two-party vote for Trump. However, Republican voter registration should have either no relationship or a negative effect in both the model of Trump's overperformance of Romney and the pivot county model. All else equal, counties with higher shares of Republican registrants should also have seen higher vote totals for Mitt Romney in 2012, thus limiting the growth potential for Trump among Republican voters in 2016.[1]

3.2   White, Working-Class Voters, the Education Gap, and Economic Anxiety

White, working-class voters were a part of the Trump narrative throughout the campaign. During the primary phase, some argued that white, working-class voters supportive of Trump were driving a "rebellion against Republican elites" (Silver 2016). During the general election, white, working-class voters were drawn to Trump because of his messaging on trade, jobs, and wages (Zitner and Overberg 2016; Casselman 2017; Wasserman 2017). White, working-class voters were also attracted to

Trump because he owned his own business and there was a perception he had created jobs and wealth throughout his business career. Additionally, these voters appreciated Trump's "straight talk," his willingness to "tell it like it is" (Williams 2016).

While there is no evidence that white, working-class voters were a particularly powerful force during the nomination stage (Silver 2016), they were an important part of Trump's winning coalition during the general election (Trende 2017). Silver (2017a) called white voters without a college degree Trump's "strongest demographic group."[2] Trump's support among white voters was strong (57%-37%), but his support among those without a college degree was even stronger. Trump won white voters without a college degree 66%-29% (Exit Polls 2016a). Trump also won white women without a college degree 61%-34%, a significant loss for Hillary Clinton, who needed the votes of white women to win key states (Malone 2016). Trump's support in Iowa among white, working-class voters mirrored that of the national electorate (Exit Polls 2016b). He won white voters 54% to Clinton's 40%. He not only won whites with a college degree (49%-44%), he also won whites without a college degree 58% to Clinton's 38%. In doing so, Trump was able to win counties in eastern Iowa, which had been Democratic strongholds for decades (Cohen and Simon 2016).

The education gap in 2016 highlights an important change in the relationship between race, education, and partisan identification over time, particularly in the aftermath of the Obama presidency. Sides et al. (2018) document shifts in partisan identity among racial groups from 1992 through 2016. Over time, the Democratic Party "has become increasingly attractive to nonwhites and to whites with more formal education" (25). Democrats have long enjoyed advantages with African Americans, but advantages among Asian Americans and Hispanic Americans are more recent. The significant change, however, was among white Americans and this is where educational attainment enters the equation. For white Americans with a college degree, the attractiveness of the Democratic Party has grown since 1992. For white Americans without a college degree, the Democratic Party has grown less attractive over time, leading to a higher likelihood of identifying with the Republican Party. The authors argue this change is primarily driven by attitudes about race. White Americans with higher levels of educational attainment tend to hold more positive views of racial and ethnic minorities, thus the

Democratic Party becomes more attractive due to its support for more liberal policies regarding race. The assessment of racial and ethnic minorities for white Americans without a college degree is not nearly as favorable, hence the shift toward the Republican Party. This fact could explain why scholars saw support for Democratic candidates among white, working-class voters declining not only in Iowa, but also across the Midwest in the latter years of the Obama presidency (Enten 2014, 2016).

It is also important to note that white, working-class voters are disproportionately found in swing states, including Iowa. The 2016 non-Hispanic white population in Iowa accounts for 87% of all residents (U.S. Census Bureau 2017a). White Iowans represented approximately 94% of all registered voters and all actual voters in 2016 based upon the 2016 Cooperative Congressional Election Survey (Ansolabehere and Schaffner 2017). Approximately 27.1% of the entire Iowa population over the age of 25 has earned a bachelor's degree (U.S. Census Bureau 2017b). For non-Hispanic whites, 28.3% have earned at least a bachelor's degree. The overrepresentation of white, working-class voters in swing states continues to give Republicans key advantages in both presidential elections due to the Electoral College and in statewide races (Silver 2017a, b).

Economic issues were certainly on the minds of voters in 2016. Exit polls reveal that 52% of Americans and 54% of Iowans believed that the economy was the "most important issue facing the country" (Exit Polls 2016a, b). Trump's support from white, working-class voters was driven not by "economic hardship" but by "economic anxiety" (Casselman 2017). Economic hardship is a measure of a voter's current economic position. Is the individual employed? Has the individual fallen into poverty or lost a home? Economic hardship was a better predictor of support for Hillary Clinton versus Donald Trump in 2016. Using individual income as an example, Clinton fared much better with voters reporting incomes under $50,000 per year (53%-41%) than she did with those earning over $50,000 per year (Trump 48%-Clinton 47%). The gap was magnified even more in Iowa. Her vote share in the former income bracket was 52%, but Trump actually won those with incomes over $50,000 by 12% (53%-41%). It is apparent that economic anxiety or economic fears about the future drove support for Trump. For example, Casselman found that slow job growth was associated with support for Trump. He also discovered that as subprime loans or disability payments increased, or earnings decreased, support for Trump increased at the county level.

Three measures were included in the modeling to assess the impact of white, working-class voters; educational attainment; and economic anxiety on county-level support for Trump. First, the percentage of non-Hispanic white county residents over the age of 25 who had earned a bachelor's degree or higher was included (U.S. Census Bureau 2017b). This measure serves as the primary proxy for the white, working-class population in Iowa. A higher percentage of residents who have earned a bachelor's degree would signify a lower proportion of white, working-class voters in the county and thus should be negatively associated with support for Trump.

Second, the change in adjusted median household income from 2000 to 2016 for each county was included (U.S. Census Bureau 2002a, 2017c). The measure was created by inflating the 2000 measure of median household income to 2016 U.S. dollars.[3] Next, the change in adjusted household income was created by subtracting the adjusted 2000 measure from the 2016 measure and then dividing by the 2000 measure. This formula creates a measure of economic insecurity since, instead of measuring income within each county, the longitudinal change in purchasing power for each county is measured. A negative value on the measure would indicate a decline in purchasing power over the 16-year period either due to declining wages or a loss of purchasing power as a result of rising prices and a failure of wages in keeping pace. A positive value would indicate an increase in purchasing power over the same period. If economic anxiety was a factor for voters in 2016, the relationship between the change in adjusted median household income measure and support for Trump should be negative.

Third, the change in the percentage of residents employed in manufacturing from 2000 to 2016 was included for each county as well (U.S. Census Bureau 2002a, 2017c). This measure was also created by subtracting the 2000 measure from the 2016 measure and then dividing by the 2000 measure. The measure would be sensitive to any manufacturing job losses over the 16-year period, but it would also be sensitive to any growth in manufacturing jobs for county residents, too. A negative value on the measure would indicate that fewer county residents were employed in manufacturing in 2016 than in 2000. A positive value would indicate growth in manufacturing jobs across the county. Like the change in adjusted household income measure, the change in manufacturing jobs is a measure of economic anxiety; as a result, it should be negatively associated with Trump support.

3.3 RACE AND IDENTITY

Race and identity were also important factors in the 2016 presidential campaign. There were questions during the campaign regarding how racial and ethnic minorities would respond to the candidacies of Clinton and Trump. Would racial and ethnic minorities, identified early on as core elements of a winning coalition for Clinton, turn out and support Clinton as they did for Barack Obama in 2008 and 2012? Would the harsh rhetoric on immigration and Muslims result in Trump underperforming Mitt Romney with racial and ethnic minorities?

At the national level, little changed in terms of the voter turnout of racial and ethnic minorities. The turnout of African Americans as a share of the electorate dropped slightly from 13% in 2012 to 12% in 2016 (Exit Polls 2012a, 2016a). However, the share of the electorate that was Hispanic or Asian increased by 1%. In Iowa, the turnout rates of African Americans (2%) and Asians (1%) remained the same from 2012 to 2016, but Hispanic turnout in Iowa increased from 2% in 2012 to 5% in 2016 (Exit Polls 2012b, 2016b). In terms of vote share, Trump outperformed Mitt Romney in 2016 with racial and ethnic minorities nationally, although the gains were modest. His support among African Americans was 2% higher than Romney's in 2012 (8%-6%). He received 28% of the Hispanic vote versus Romney's 27% in 2012 and received 27% of the Asian vote versus Romney's 26%. In Iowa, Trump secured 26% of the Hispanic vote in 2016.[4]

To some, Trump's performance among Hispanic voters was puzzling in light of Trump's rhetoric on immigration and Mexicans. His performance, however, was consistent with Republican presidential candidates' performance over the last few decades when examining the normalized Hispanic vote share, which shows that Hispanic voters are slowly moving toward the Republican Party. Trende (2017) believes there are three reasons why Trump did better than expected with Hispanics. First, he posits that Republican candidates most likely have a vote share floor of around 25% with Hispanics. Second, he cites polling data which shows the issue of immigration is not nearly as salient among Hispanic voters as other issues happen to be. Third, Hispanic voters are more likely than African Americans to move toward the Republican Party as they accrue wealth.

Attitudes about race and identity also appear to have played a role in how white voters made decisions in the 2016 election. Sides, Tesler, and Vavreck (2018, 7) argue that both Hillary Clinton and Donald Trump "helped 'activate' ethnic identities and attitudes, thereby making them more strongly related to what ordinary Americans thought and how they voted." This helped prime white voters to view political choices in 2016 through the lens of race and identity. Enos (2017, 139) posits that immigrants, particularly Mexican immigrants, have become "the bogeyman of American politics," often being used as a "convenient scapegoat for problems" such as crime, drugs, and job loss by "conservative politicians." Research on the 2016 election found that anti-immigrant sentiment was strongly associated with support for Trump (Drutman 2017; McElwee and McDaniel 2017; Rapoport and Stone 2017; Hooghe and Dassonneville 2018) and vote switching from Obama in 2012 to Trump in 2016 (Reny et al. 2019). Researchers have also found that racial attitudes such as "racial resentment," "racism denial," "racial status threat," and "white group consciousness" were significant predictors of Trump support in 2016, even explaining significant portions of the education gap seen in aggregate-level analyses and reducing the predictive power of economic anxiety in explaining individual-level support for Trump (Abramowitz 2017; Mutz 2018; Schaffner et al. 2018; Abramowitz and McCoy 2019).

Theoretically, there is reason to believe that anti-immigrant sentiment, or a growing resistance to the nonwhite population, may have played a role in explaining Trump's support in Iowa during 2016. First, immigration was a salient issue for Iowa voters (Hardy 2016). In Iowa exit polls, immigration was identified as the third "most important issue facing the country," only trailing the economy and terrorism (Exit Polls 2016b). For those voters, 80% voted for Trump. Additionally, there was evidence in the survey of county party officials that immigration was a very important issue, particularly for Trump voters. Respondents to the survey were asked several questions regarding issues important to both Trump and Clinton voters. Two were open-ended questions asking the respondent to identify the three most important issues for Trump or Clinton voters. The other two were closed-ended questions where respondents were provided a list of issues and asked to rate the importance of issues to Trump or Clinton voters. Figure 3.1 shows the results of the open-ended question for Trump voters in the form of a word cloud. Immigration was the most frequent response across the three issues ($N = 34$), followed by the economy ($N = 26$). In identifying immigration as an important issue, respondents used the words "build the wall," "illegal immigration," "Mexicans," "immigrant fear," and "immigration reform." On the closed-ended item, the average score for the importance of the immigration issue was 4.57, falling between "Important" and "Very Important."

Fig. 3.1 Most important issues to Donald Trump voters according to county party officials, 2016

Second, Iowa's nonwhite population has grown significantly since 2000. According to U.S. Census Bureau (2002b, 2017a) data, the average county-level growth rate for nonwhite Iowans is 114.3%, ranging from 29.6% to 258.0%. Lay (2012) notes the growth rate for Hispanic residents was 170% statewide from 1990 to 2000, which ranked eleventh nationally and third in the Midwest. While Lay found that tolerance for immigrants increased over time in rural Iowa communities, other studies indicate that rural Americans are more likely to hold negative views of immigrants than urban or suburban Americans (Fennelly and Federico 2008). Furthermore, growth in the immigrant population can lead to rising levels of anti-immigrant sentiment in communities when political elites make the issue of immigration salient (Hopkins 2010). This finding may partially explain why Trump's overperformance of Romney was largest in counties that experienced the largest growth in Hispanic population from 2000 to 2014 (Enos 2017).

In assessing the impact of race and identity, the change in the percentage of nonwhites from 2000 to 2016 for each county was included. This measure was created by subtracting the nonwhite county-level population in 2000 from the nonwhite county-level population in 2016 and then dividing by the 2000 measure. Instead of measuring the size of the nonwhite population in each county, this variable measures the size of the growth in the nonwhite population. The expectation is that the measure would be positively associated with support for Trump in 2016, or Trump support should be higher in counties where increased growth in the nonwhite population occurred.

3.4   THE RURAL–URBAN DIVIDE

The key to understanding the outcome of the 2016 election in Iowa may lie in understanding the rural–urban divide across the state. In 2010, about 36% of Iowa's population lived in what the U.S. Census Bureau defines as "rural areas" (U.S. Census Bureau 2015). According to Census data aggregated by the Iowa State Data Center, the population in rural Iowa is on the decline. In 1980, 41.4% of Iowans lived in rural areas, 39.4% in 1990, and 38.9% in 2000 (ISDC n.d.). Rural voters made up 17% of all voters nationwide in 2016 (Exit Polls 2016a). In Iowa, rural voters made up 39% of all voters (Exit Polls 2016b). Rural voters, both nationally and in Iowa, were more likely to support Donald Trump. Nationally, 61% of rural voters cast a ballot for Trump, while 63% of rural Iowa voters did the same. So, why were rural voters more likely to support Trump?

Part of the answer probably lies in how rural Americans view politics, government, and the political parties. Katherine Cramer (2016a), in her book on rural Wisconsin, develops a concept she refers to as "rural consciousness." Rural consciousness is much more than a simple identification with the rural place where they live:

> It includes a sense that decision makers routinely ignore rural places and fail to give rural communities their fair share of resources, as well as a sense that rural folks are fundamentally different from urbanites in terms of lifestyles, values, and work ethic. Rural consciousness signals an identification with rural people and rural places and denotes a multifaceted resentment against cities. (5–6)

Fundamentally, it means that many rural Americans feel left behind by government. They believe politicians do not listen to them or care about issues that are important to them. They believe their tax dollars go into the state (or federal) treasury and then are not equitably sent back for expenditure in rural areas. They believe urban residents have distinct advantages that are not available in rural areas, and they blame government because of the notion that government favors urban communities while neglecting rural ones. As a result, many rural Americans do not trust state government, nor do they trust the federal government (Wuthnow 2018). Rural folks also do not trust politicians whom they associate with the "establishment." Therefore, when faced with a choice between Donald Trump, the outsider, and Hillary Clinton, the establishment candidate, they chose the outsider (DBR n.d.). There is evidence in the qualitative data discussed in Chap. 2 which supports this conclusion in Iowa.

Additionally, some argue that the strategy developed by Clinton's campaign team ignored rural Iowa, including many respondents to the survey of county party officials and state political elites interviewed. One reason: Assumptions about the electorate in 2016. Polls of the electorate in the spring of 2016 led some to believe "the electorate would look much like the one in 2012" (Barone 2016). Democrats assumed rural voters, who had turned out for Barack Obama in 2008 and 2012, would do so once again. Others believed Clinton's lack of outreach to rural areas was a function of the campaign's perception that they did not need rural voters to win, banking on their strategy to run up vote margins in largely urban areas across the country. As a result, the campaign did not develop nearly as large of an operation in rural states like Iowa, even though some, like former Governor Tom Vilsack, "urged the Clinton campaign to shore up rural outreach" (Evich 2016).

Not only do rural Americans feel left behind by government and the establishment, they also feel left behind by the global economy as well. In 2016, many rural voters were looking for a message of economic hope and prosperity. As mentioned above, 54% of Iowa voters believed the economy was the "most important issue facing the economy" (Exit Polls 2016b). Trump delivered this message. He talked about bad trade deals and how he was going to bring manufacturing back. He talked about job and wage growth. He talked about deregulating the economy to help businesses flourish. Coupled with his brash style and outsider position, Trump's message resonated in rural America (Longworth 2016). Rural voters saw "hope" in Trump's message. In fact, one Democratic respondent to the survey said, "I know this sounds crazy. Obama won in 2012 with his key word, HOPE. HOPE won for Trump in 2016." Rural voters listened, and rural voters showed up on Election Day to vote for Donald Trump.

To assess the impact of a county being a rural or urban, the Rural–Urban Continuum Code (RUCC) for each county was included (USDA-ERS 2013). Developed by the Economic Research Service at the U.S. Department of Agriculture, the codes range from a score of 1 to 9, of which eight are applicable to Iowa. The first three values represent counties in metropolitan areas, split by population. Metro counties with greater than one million residents are coded 1. Metro counties with

250,000 to 1,000,000 residents are coded 2. Metro counties with up to 250,000 residents are coded 3. The remaining categories represent counties that fall outside of the metropolitan areas of a state, but they also take into account whether the county is adjacent to a metro area: Counties adjacent to a metropolitan area with greater than 20,000 residents in cities are coded 4 and those not adjacent to a metropolitan area are coded 5. Counties that are adjacent to a metropolitan area with 2500 to 19,999 residents in cities are coded 6 and those not adjacent to a metropolitan area are coded 7. Finally, counties adjacent to a metropolitan area with city populations of less than 2500 are coded 8 and those not adjacent to a metropolitan area are coded 9.

While some may advocate for measures of total county population to serve as a proxy for the rural–urban divide, the RUCC provides a more refined measure of rural versus urban because it accounts for metropolitan status and proximity of non-metro counties to metro areas. Consider, for example, Mills County in southwest Iowa. In 2016, Mills County had an estimated population of 14,972 (U.S. Census Bureau 2017a). In terms of population, it ranks 47th out of Iowa's 99 counties. However, its proximity to the Omaha metropolitan area leads to its RUCC code of 2. It is important to take population and metropolitan status into account, as proximity to a metropolitan area gives residents certain advantages that similarly sized counties cannot enjoy. Closer proximity to metropolitan areas can lead to greater access to both improved educational opportunities to develop essential skills and improved economic opportunities. Closer proximity to metropolitan areas affords some smaller counties the opportunity to attract new residents employed in larger cities who want to live in a smaller, more rural community. The use of the RUCC takes all of these elements into account. It is also reasonable to believe proximity to a metropolitan area might cause political differences as well, meaning that political outcomes could differ across the eight categories of the RUCC. It is expected that outcomes will vary across the eight categories, and the RUCC will be positively associated with Trump support. In other words, as counties become more rural, support for Trump will increase.

3.5   Evangelical Christian Voters

Evangelical Christians were also an integral part of Trump's winning electoral coalition. In the waning days of the primary campaign, some wondered if Trump could coalesce evangelical support in the general election.

He has been married three times. He owns casinos. He does not believe he needs to ask God for forgiveness. He has voiced lewd and demeaning comments about women (Zoll 2016). Any of these facts would have been disqualifying in past Republican primary contests or general elections for evangelicals. Evangelicals, however, stuck with Trump in 2016. Nationally, 80% of all evangelical voters voted for Trump while in Iowa, 70% of evangelicals backed Trump (Exit Polls 2016a, b).

Researchers have been studying Trump's share of the evangelical vote since the 2016 election, and they have offered an array of reasons why evangelicals supported him. Posner (2017) argues that some white evangelicals were attracted to Trump's racially charged rhetoric regarding immigrants and Muslims. Others argue that Trump's support among the evangelical community is driven by his support for religious liberty, his pro-life position on abortion, and his assurance that he would appoint conservative jurists to the bench (Stewart 2016; Zoll 2016). This argument also found support among the Iowa political elites who participated in interviews and throughout the survey of county party officials. Six of the eight statewide elites believed Trump's list of potential Supreme Court nominees, released during the summer of 2016, helped ease any concerns that evangelical Christians or establishment Republicans had about voting for Trump. Readers also should note the prominence of the words "abortion" and "scotus" in Fig. 3.1, which highlight how important those issues were to Trump voters in Iowa according to county party officials. Abortion ($\mu = 4.27$) and Supreme Court appointments ($\mu = 4.24$) also ranked high in terms of issue importance for Trump voters.

Ultimately, evangelicals behaved like they have for decades: Like Republicans. Jones (2016) notes evangelicals "unevenly yoked themselves to the party of Reagan in reaction to the civil rights movement in the 1980s." According to a survey of evangelical voters by the Billy Graham Center Institute at Wheaton College in 2018, respondents were more likely to list more secular issues such as the economy, health care, or immigration as reasons for their vote in 2016. Religious liberty and abortion ranked lower not only when respondents were asked to identify the "most important factor" but also when they were asked "to list *any* factors that influenced their 2016 vote" (Stetzer and MacDonald 2018). Their conclusion: "Republican Party issues were more important than pro-life issues."

In Iowa, Christian conservatives have long been tied to the Republican Party of Iowa.[5] Dating back to the early 1980s, evangelical Christians have supported other conservatives within the party to ensure the party does not move too far toward the ideological center (Racheter et al. 2003). Evangelicals have served in prominent positions within the formal party organization and have been influential in shaping the party's platform. Evangelical Protestants have also been a core constituency of Republican candidates running for office at all levels, from the state legislature to the presidency (Conger and Racheter 2006). A county-level analysis of the Republican presidential vote in Iowa from 1980 through 2000 revealed the evangelical population of the county was the most powerful predictor of the Republican presidential vote in every election except for 1980, when it was the second-most powerful predictor (Racheter et al. 2003). In 2016, an individual-level analysis predicting a vote for Donald Trump also showed evangelicals as much more likely to support Trump than non-evangelicals (Larimer and Hoffman 2018).

To assess the impact of the evangelical Christian population on support for Trump at the county level, the percentage of the county population defined as evangelical Protestant was included (ASARB 2010). The expectation is the measure will be positively associated with Trump's share of the two-party vote. However, like the measure for Republican registrants, the share of evangelicals for each county should either not be associated with or negatively associated with Trump's overperformance of Mitt Romney and whether the county pivoted in 2016 from Barack Obama to Trump. If evangelicals are truly a core constituency of Republican candidates, support in a two-candidate race should increase. But, in the case of overperformance, the expectation would be that Romney performed well with evangelicals in 2012, leaving little room for growth among evangelical voters.

Assessing county-level support for Donald Trump included the use of three dependent variables.[6] The first dependent variable used was Trump's share of the two-party vote for each county (IA SOS 2016a). Second, the same predictors were used to predict Trump's overperformance of Mitt Romney in 2012 for each county. To calculate the dependent variable, Romney's share of the two-party vote in 2012 was subtracted from Trump's 2016 two-party share (IA SOS 2012). The final dependent variable used was whether or not the county was a pivot county in 2016. There were 32 counties in Iowa that pivoted from Barack Obama in 2012 to Trump in 2016.[7]

3.6   Predicting Donald Trump's Share of the Two-Party Vote in 2016

Using the word "large" to describe Trump's share of the two-party vote in Iowa would be an understatement. His average county-level share was 64.6% and ranged from 29.5% in Johnson County in southeast Iowa to 86.5% in Sioux County in northwest Iowa. The distribution of the data around the mean is fairly normal, with the middle half of the counties falling between 60.2% and 71.2%. Even Johnson County, although more than 13 points lower than the next lowest case (Story County at 43.1%), is not considered an outlier as it falls within three standard deviations of the mean.

Figure 3.2 graphically depicts the bivariate relationships between the seven predictors and Trump's share of the two-party vote. The relationship between the predictors and the dependent variable is in the expected direction for six of the seven predictors, and the correlation coefficients for six of the seven predictors are statistically significant. Even though the relationship between change in manufacturing employment and Trump's vote share is negative as expected, the correlation coefficient ($r = -0.10$)

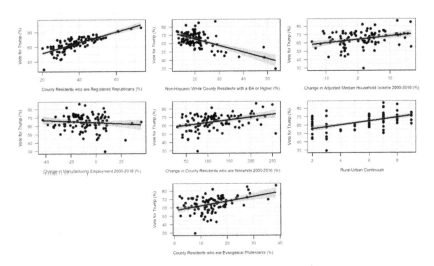

Fig. 3.2   Donald Trump's two-party vote share by county-level predictors, 2016

fails to reach statistical significance. Contrary to expectations, the correlation coefficient for change in adjusted median household income is positive ($r = 0.31$) and is statistically significant, indicating that counties with higher levels of income growth are associated with higher levels of Trump support.

The relationships between the remaining predictors and Trump's vote share are in the expected direction and are statistically significant. The associations between the five predictors and support for Trump reflect modest to strong relationships. The "weakest" correlation is between change in the nonwhite population and support for Trump ($r = 0.37$). The strongest association is between Republican registrants and Trump support ($r = 0.77$). The remaining correlations fall somewhere between ±0.4 and ±0.6. Of particular note are the correlation coefficients for educational attainment (the proxy for white, working-class voters) and rural–urban status. Both are in the expected direction and both have correlations that exceed ±0.5 ($r = -0.58$ and 0.52, respectively), showing some support for the idea that white, working-class voters and rural voters were more likely to support Trump in 2016.

The results of the multivariate model are presented in Table 3.1. The predictors combine to explain a substantial amount of the variation in county-level vote share for Trump (84.3%). The relationships between six of the seven predictors and the dependent variable are in the expected direction, and four of the seven predictors are statistically significant.

Table 3.1   Predicting Donald Trump's share of the two-party vote, 2016

Predictor	OLS coefficient	Standard error
Republican voters (%)	0.539***	0.049
College degree (%)	−0.579***	0.067
Change in adjusted median household income (%)	0.122*	0.060
Change in manufacturing employment (%)	−0.034	0.029
Change in nonwhite population (%)	0.014[a]	0.008
Rural–Urban continuum	0.372	0.226
Evangelical Protestants (%)	0.155*	0.064
Intercept	49.994***	2.795
$N =$	99	
$R^2 =$	0.843	

Note: Modeled using lm() function in R
[a]$p < 0.1$, *$p < 0.05$, **$p < 0.01$, ***$p < 0.001$

Change in manufacturing employment, while in the predicted direction, was not statistically significant. Neither was the rural–urban continuum measure. The measure of change in the nonwhite population was in the predicted direction and marginally significant ($p = 0.095$). This result could be due to Trump's unexpected performance with racial and ethnic minority voters in 2016, or it could possibly be the result of negative sentiment toward nonwhites by white voters. Change in household income is the only variable with a sign that runs counter to the prediction discussed above. Its positive sign and coefficient indicate that, as the change in adjusted median household income of a county increases, Trump's vote share increased as well. While this measure was intended to be a measure of economic anxiety (hence the prediction of a negative relationship), it is probably positive due to Trump's success in attracting more affluent voters (a core constituent group for Republican candidates) to his coalition, as exit polls indicated that Trump fared much better with more affluent voters than Hillary Clinton did (Exit Polls 2016b).

The remaining three predictors were in the predicted direction and were statistically significant. There is evidence in the model suggesting that Trump was able to successfully coalesce Republican and evangelical voters, which were both important cohorts that Trump needed to win to defeat Hillary Clinton in Iowa. Both predictors were positive, meaning that an increase in the proportion of Republican registrants or evangelical voters is associated with an increase in the two-party vote for Trump. An increase of one standard deviation in the percentage of Republican voters within a county leads to a 5.3% increase in average vote share for Trump. The relationship between the proportion of evangelicals in a county and Trump's vote share is weaker yet significant: A one standard deviation increase in the percentage of evangelical Protestants in a county leads to a 1.1% increase in Trump's two-party vote share. Additionally, there is evidence of an education gap in the model. The proxy for white, working-class voters (i.e., the percentage of county residents with a college degree) was negative and statistically significant, showing that as the proportion of residents with a college degree goes up, Trump's vote share, on average, decreases. Substantively, an increase of one standard deviation in the education variable leads to a 4% decrease in Trump's vote share. Overall, the model suggests that Donald Trump was able to combine core Republican voters with white, working-class voters to maximize his two-party vote share in Iowa.

3.7   PREDICTING VOTE SHIFTS IN 2016

One of the most fascinating aspects of Trump's victory in Iowa was his overperformance of Mitt Romney. Statewide, Trump received 70,366 more votes in 2016 than Romney did in 2012, which translates to 8.1% more votes (IA SOS 2012; 2016a). It is also true Hillary Clinton underperformed Barack Obama in 2016 by 168,875 votes statewide. Trump's overperformance averaged 12.43% across all 99 counties ranging from −2.3% in Johnson County to 21.6% in Howard County. Howard County, in northeast Iowa, is the only county in America that had a 20%+ margin for both Obama in 2012 and Trump in 2016 (Wasserman 2017). Trump only underperformed Romney in two counties (Johnson and Dallas Counties), and overperformed Romney by 15% or more in 29 counties. The "Trump overperformance of Romney" variable is distributed fairly well with the middle half of the data falling between 10.5% and 15.3%. While not a perfect proxy for vote switching in 2016, it does encompass some of the reshuffling in the electorate between 2012 and 2016.

With the exception of two predictors, the correlation coefficients between the predictors and the overperformance measure are much smaller than they were when examining the association with Trump's share of the two-party vote. All seven correlations are in the predicted direction, but only two reach acceptable levels of statistical significance: Percentage of white residents with a college degree ($r = -0.87$) and Rural–Urban Continuum ($r = 0.53$). The correlation coefficient for evangelical Protestants ($r = -0.17$) is marginally significant ($p = 0.09$). At the bivariate level, this suggests that a higher level of overperformance by Trump was associated with rural counties having larger shares of white, working-class voters.

When controlling for the other predictors in the model, the presence of an education gap and whether the county is rural or urban shapes the magnitude of Trump's overperformance of Romney in 2016 (Table 3.2). The predictors combined explain 84% of the variance on the overperformance measure. Five of the seven predictors are in the expected direction and four of the predictors are statistically significant. Of the predictors that are not in the expected direction (change in adjusted median household income and change in the nonwhite population), neither reaches acceptable levels of statistical significance.

Table 3.2 Predicting Donald Trump's overperformance of Mitt Romney, 2016

Predictor	OLS coefficient	Standard error
Republican voters (%)	−0.108***	0.023
College degree (%)	−0.502***	0.031
Change in adjusted median household income (%)	0.042	0.028
Change in manufacturing employment (%)	−0.010	0.014
Change in nonwhite population (%)	−0.002	0.004
Rural–Urban continuum	0.414***	0.106
Evangelical Protestants (%)	−0.065*	0.030
Intercept	25.732***	1.308
$N =$	99	
$R^2 =$	0.841	

Note: Modeled using lm() function in R
$*p < 0.05$, $**p < 0.01$, $***p < 0.001$

Consistent with expectations, the share of Republican voters and the proportion of evangelical Protestants within a county are negatively related to Trump's overperformance of Romney. It certainly was expected that Republican registration and percentage of evangelicals in a county would be positively related to Trump's vote total, but both factors were positively related to Romney's vote total in 2012 as well. As a result, Trump had little room to grow his vote share among both core constituencies. When examining the relationship between Trump's overperformance, Romney's 2012 vote share, and Republican registrants or share of evangelicals, the growth potential is clear. In Fig. 3.3, Romney's share of the two-party vote is plotted on the horizontal axis, and the size of Trump's overperformance of the 2012 vote for Romney is plotted on the vertical axis. The size of the point in the plot is based upon the size of the Republican voter base in the top panel and the size of the evangelical population in the bottom panel. As you move from left to right on the horizontal axis, the size of Romney's vote share increases. However, also notice the size of the Republican voter base and the size of the evangelical population increase as well. Additionally, the size of Trump's margin over Romney trends downward when moving from left to right. This suggests Trump's growth potential was not within counties where Romney did exceptionally well (i.e., counties with high proportions of Republican and evangelical voters) but rather within counties with lower shares of Republicans and evangelical voters.[8]

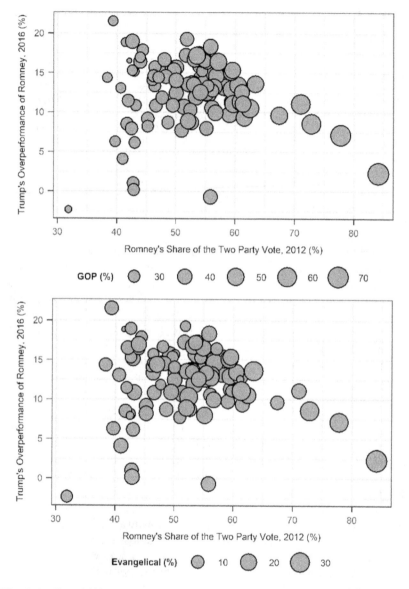

Fig. 3.3 Donald Trump's overperformance of Mitt Romney by Romney's share of the two-party vote by Republican voter registration and evangelical Christians

Where was Trump's overperformance the highest? The short answer: In rural counties with a larger share of white, working-class voters. First, Trump performed better vis-à-vis Mitt Romney in more rural counties. At the bivariate level, Trump overperformed Romney, on average, by 8.5% in the largest metropolitan areas of the state. In the most rural portions of the state (counties with less than 2500 residents living in cities and not adjacent to a metropolitan area), Trump's overperformance was 16.1% on average. When holding the other predictors constant at their means, Trump's average overperformance in the largest metropolitan counties was 10.8%. In the most rural, 13.7%. There is also some evidence at the bivariate level suggesting that a county's adjacency to a metro area matters. For counties with a population of 20,000 or more, the average score on the overperformance measure was 11.7% (for counties adjacent to a metro area) and 14.4% (for counties not adjacent to a metro area), respectively. There is a consistent pattern for the most rural counties as well.[9]

Second, Trump's overperformance, on average, was larger in counties with larger shares of white, working-class voters. The negative coefficient indicates that, as the share of college educated whites increases in a county, Trump's overperformance of Romney goes down. Statistically, a decrease of one standard deviation in the percentage of white county residents with a college degree leads to a 3.5% increase in Trump's overperformance. With the educational attainment predictor and the remaining predictors set at their mean values, Trump's overperformance of Romney averages 12.4%. A decrease of one standard deviation of educational attainment leads to an average overperformance score of 15.9%. Overall, the results of the Trump overperformance model suggest that Trump's overperformance was not a function of increased support from Republicans and evangelicals. It was most likely a function of how rural and white, working-class voters viewed the two Republican candidates across the two election cycles and how these views shaped their decision to vote and whom to vote for. The results also suggest a large number of Iowa's vote switchers resided in more rural counties and were less likely to have a college degree.

Another way to look at vote switching at the county level is to examine the likelihood of a county being a pivot county in 2016. Pivot counties, as discussed in Chap. 1, were counties won by Barack Obama in 2012 but then flipped to Donald Trump in 2016. There were 32 pivot counties in the state, most of which fell in eastern Iowa (see Fig. 1.2). In western Iowa, only Boone, Clarke, Union, Webster, and Woodbury Counties pivoted from Obama to Trump in 2016. Obama's margins in those five western

Table 3.3   Predicting whether a county was a pivot county, 2016

Predictor	Logistic coefficient	Standard error
Republican voters (%)	−0.306***	0.078
College degree (%)	−0.195**	0.071
Change in adjusted median household income (%)	−0.053	0.052
Change in manufacturing employment (%)	0.001	0.023
Change in nonwhite population (%)	0.002	0.007
Rural–Urban continuum	−0.140	0.193
Evangelical Protestants (%)	−0.168*	0.066
Intercept	16.762***	4.228
N =	99	
χ^2 =	62.713***	
McFadden's R^2 =	0.503	

Note: Modeled using glm (family = binomial) function in R
*$p < 0.05$, **$p < 0.01$, ***$p < 0.001$

Iowa counties were very small, ranging from 1.04% in Woodbury County to 6.8% in Boone County (IA SOS 2012). The remaining 27 pivot counties fell across eastern Iowa. Obama's average margin in the 27 pivot counties in eastern Iowa was 11.72%, ranging from 0.7% in Louisa County to 23.2% in Clinton County. A binary logistic regression model was run to predict whether or not a county was a pivot county in 2016, using the same seven predictors used to predict Trump's 2016 vote share and Trump's overperformance of Romney. If status as a pivot county is a county-level proxy for vote switching, the results from the logistic regression model should be similar to those of the preceding model of Trump's overperformance (Table 3.3).[10]

The results are indeed similar yet not identical. Once again, six of the seven predictors are in the anticipated direction. The only predictor not in the expected direction is the rural–urban continuum measure. However, it is not statistically significant. This result is a change from the previous model of vote switching, where the rural–urban status of the county shaped Trump's overperformance in Iowa counties. Instead, it suggests that rural–urban status did not play a role in explaining the likelihood of a county switching from Obama to Trump in 2016. Conversely, it is possible that the variable flipping signs and falling out of statistical significance in the pivot county model may be a function of the association between educational attainment and rural–urban status. The correlation between the two variables is moderately high ($r = −0.52$), which could possibly be masking the effect of rural–urban status in the results.[11]

Of the remaining six predictors, three are statistically significant and help explain the probability of being a pivot county in 2016. Two of the three predictors, share of Republican voters and the proportion of the county that is evangelical Protestant, are negative. This result means that the probability of being a pivot county in 2016 decreases as the predictor increases. Similar to the findings of the Trump overperformance model, this result is not surprising. Counties with higher shares of Republican voters and evangelical Christians represented core voters for Mitt Romney in 2012, so there was little to no room for growth within these populations. In other words, Romney did very well in many of the non-pivot counties, winning 61 of 67. As a result, one would expect the probability of a county shifting from Obama to Trump to decrease in counties with more Republican and evangelical voters.

The educational attainment variable is the most important predictor to look at in the model. It is negative and statistically significant ($p < 0.01$). The coefficient reveals that the probability of a county becoming a pivot county in 2016 increased as the percentage of white residents with a college degree decreased. When holding the other six predictors constant at their mean values, the probability of a being a pivot county for a county with an average level of educational attainment (21.1% with college degrees) is 0.114. Counties with an educational attainment one standard deviation below the mean (approximately 14% with college degrees) have about a one-in-three chance of being a pivot county (0.331). There is a 3% chance of being a pivot county for counties with an educational attainment one standard deviation above the mean (approximately 28% with college degrees) and there is a 0.9% chance for counties with an educational attainment two standard deviations about the mean (approximately 35% with college degrees). Overall, this model suggests that counties pivoting from Barack Obama in 2012 to Donald Trump in 2016 was not necessarily a function of rural versus urban. Rather, it was a function of educational attainment: Counties with higher shares of white, working-class voters were much more likely to swing from Obama to Trump.

3.8   Conclusion

This chapter started with an epigraph about rural Iowa. It cannot be determined by the evidence presented above whether Hillary Clinton failed to show up in rural Iowa, whether her message did not resonate in rural Iowa, or whether Donald Trump's message significantly resonated in rural Iowa. However, it can be determined that Donald Trump performed very well in rural Iowa, particularly with white, working-class voters. Moving into 2016, the shift of white, working-class voters toward the Republican Party in Iowa was a relatively new trend, first noticed by Harry Enten (2014) in the aftermath of Senator Joni Ernst's election in 2014. The evidence above shows Trump was able to recognize and consolidate this new voting bloc, along with typical Republican base voters and evangelical Protestants, to build the winning coalition that propelled him to victory in Iowa.

The Trump campaign knew this voting bloc was available in 2016; and, if Trump was going to improve upon Mitt Romney's performance in 2012, they needed to win these "hidden Trump voters," who were "largely white, disengaged, and non-urban" (Evich 2016). The Trump campaign speculated the key to electing Trump as president would be to maximize turnout in rural areas. They knew the potential was there; it was just a matter of turning out the voters. They saw this "silent majority" turn out in even larger numbers than the campaign could have predicted. The evidence above shows that Trump's campaign was successful in bringing these rural voters into the fold significantly building upon Romney's performance all across Iowa. Furthermore, Trump overperformed Romney in 32 of the 38 states won by Barack Obama in 2012. Political polling during the campaign largely missed how sizable this group of voters really was, not only in Iowa but across rural America. In the aftermath of the campaign, Katherine Cramer (2016b) revisited two of the groups she worked with while writing her book on rural Wisconsin. They explained to her they "didn't just ignore, but actively lied to, pollsters" in the lead up to the November election, which would have underestimated rural support for Trump in the November election.

It is never wise to infer individual-level causality from aggregate-level data, but it is clear there was something about Trump's candidacy that resonated with not only traditional Republican voters and evangelical Protestants, but also among large numbers of white, working-class voters from rural areas of the state. To this end, there is a clear education gap in the county-level results presented above. The question is, why? Why did Trump resonate with this class of voters in Iowa during the 2016 campaign? What is it about rural white, working-class voters that explains the sharp differences from their urban counterparts? We turn to these questions in Chap. 4.

NOTES

1. Ideally, the modeling would have included the share of active Independent, or No Party voters as they are called in Iowa. The share of active No Party voters was excluded for two reasons. First, without individual-level data or a comprehensive study of Iowa's No Party voters to cite, we cannot theoretically understand the linkage between the share of No Party voters and Trump's share of the two-party vote. Iowa's No Party voters could be centrists. They also could also be partisan leaners. Since we do not know, it was important to exclude the measure. Second, the association between the share of active Republican registrants and the share of active No Party registrants is negative and statistically significant ($r = -0.68$). What this demonstrates is that counties with large shares of active Republican voters are less likely to have a robust share of No Party voters. It is more likely, however, for counties to have robust shares of both active Democratic and No Party voters. When both variables (Republican and No Party) are modeled together as explanatory variables of Trump's share of the two-party vote, the sign for both variables is positive. However, the correlation between the share of active No Party Registrants and Trump's two-party vote is negative and statistically significant ($r = -0.35$). The regression result is spurious as controlling for counties with larger shares of Republican voters simply picks up what is going on in counties with higher shares of active Democratic voters, thus not providing a reliable and valid examination of the behaviors of Iowa's No Party voters. Hoffman and Larimer (2015) found a similar pattern between active Democratic, Republican, and No Party voters in voter registration data from 2014.
2. For the purposes of this chapter, educational attainment (i.e., less than a college degree) is used as a proxy for defining white, working-class voters. While not a perfect proxy for class, data on educational attainment is readily available and is a good predictor of current employment and future job prospects. For a more detailed discussion of proxies for defining the working class, see Abramowitz and Teixeira (2009).
3. The Consumer Price Index (CPI) was used to inflate the measure from year 2000.
4. In Iowa, vote share by race was only calculated for white voters and Hispanic voters in 2016 due to the small proportion of African American and Asian voters in exit polls (Exit Polls 2016b). In 2012, it was only calculated for white voters for the same reason (Exit Polls 2012b).
5. Republican Party of Iowa Chairman Jeff Kaufmann (2019) noted in his interview that political observers from outside the state often believe evangelical Christians are the sole driving force behind the Republican Party of Iowa. Kaufmann believes the Party is much more diverse than that, including a significant group of voters who have populist preferences.

6. The full dataset and R scripts are available from the author upon request.
7. The educational attainment variable had three significant outliers. For all 99 counties, the average for the variable is 21.2% with a standard deviation of 6.9%. The three outliers were Johnson County (53.3%), Story County (48.7%), and Dallas County (48.4%). With the outliers removed, the average for the variable is 20.3% with a standard deviation of 4.7%. All three models were run with the educational attainment outliers removed to see if it substantially changed the findings. It did not. The only significant difference was for the model which predicts Trump's share of the two-party vote. In the model, the coefficients remain stable, but the change in adjusted median household income measure falls out of statistical significance, most likely because Dallas County saw the largest growth in adjusted median household income and Johnson County saw growth as well. Otherwise, the results are the same. For the other two models, all coefficients remain relatively stable and statistically significant predictors are identical except for the educational attainment variable in the pivot counties model. While its coefficient is slightly smaller, the p-value went from 0.0059 in the model with all 99 counties to 0.0505 when the outliers were removed. As a result, the two regression models and the logistic regression model reported here include all 99 counties.
8. The model was also run using Romney's share of the two-party vote in 2012 instead of the percentage of Republican registrants. The results were nearly identical, which is not surprising considering that the correlation between the share of Republican voters in 2016 and Trump's share of the two-party vote is 0.77 and the correlation between Romney's two-party vote share and Trump's two-party vote share is 0.89. Several predictors saw minor changes in the weight of their coefficients which did not impact the p-value. However, the size of the coefficient for the evangelical population decreased by 0.016 which shifted the p-value from 0.031 to 0.133. As a result, I report the model with the share of Republican registrants for consistency of predictors across the three models.
9. I hesitate to draw a definitive conclusion here for two reasons. First, the pattern does not hold for counties with urban populations between 2500 and 20,000. The average overperformance was larger for those adjacent counties versus the not adjacent counties. Second, the sample sizes in several categories are relatively small. For counties with urban populations exceeding 20,000, there are only three counties that are adjacent to metro areas and five that are not. For counties with less than 2500 urban population, there are 9 adjacent and 11 that are not.
10. For consistency with the Trump overperformance model, the logistic regression model for pivot counties uses share of Republican voters instead of Romney's share of the two-party vote in 2012. See endnote 8.

11. The latter explanation is the most likely. After rerunning the model without educational attainment in it, the coefficient for rural–urban continuum became positive, and although it did not reach statistical significance, its p-value was closer to the critical value of 0.05 ($p = 0.299$ versus $p = 0.467$).

REFERENCES

Abramowitz, Alan I. 2017. It Wasn't the Economy, Stupid: Racial Polarization, White Racial Resentment, and the Rise of Trump. In *Trumped: The 2016 Election That Broke All the Rules*, ed. Larry J. Sabato, Kyle Kondik, and Geoffrey Skelley, 202–210. Lanham, MD: Rowman & Littlefield.

Abramowitz, Alan, and Jennifer McCoy. 2019. United States: Racial Resentment, Negative Partisanship, and Polarization in Trump's America. *Annals of the American Academy of Political and Social Science* 681 (1): 137–156. https://doi.org/10.1177%2F0002716218811309.

Abramowitz, Alan, and Ruy Teixeira. 2009. The Decline of the White Working Class and the Rise of a Mass Upper-Middle Class. *Political Science Quarterly* 124 (3): 391–422. https://doi.org/10.1002/j.1538-165X.2009.tb00653.x.

Abramowitz, Alan I., and Steven Webster. 2016. The Rise of Negative Partisanship and the Nationalization of U.S. Elections in the 21st Century. *Electoral Studies* 41: 12–22. https://doi.org/10.1016/j.electstud.2015.11.001.

Ansolabehere, Stephen, and Brian F. Schaffner. 2017. *Cooperative Congressional Election Study, 2016: Common Content.* [Computer File] Release 2: August 4, 2017. Cambridge, MA: Harvard University. [Producer]. http://cces.gov.harvard.edu.

Association of Statisticians of American Religious Bodies (ASARB). 2010. 2010 U.S. Religion Census: Religious Congregations & Membership Study. Distributed by the Association of Religion Data Archives. http://www.thearda.com/ql2010/QL_C_2010_1_27p.asp.

Barone, Michael. 2016. Donald Trump and the Outstate Midwest Redraw the Partisan Lines. *Washington Examiner*, November 30. https://www.washingtonexaminer.com/trump-and-the-outstate-midwest-redraw-the-partisan-lines.

Branstad, Eric. 2018. Interview by Author. *Des Moines*, December 13.

Byler, David. 2017. How Trump Picked the Democratic Lock and Won the Presidency. In *Trumped: The 2016 Election That Broke All the Rules*, ed. Larry J. Sabato, Kyle Kondik, and Geoffrey Skelley, 30–51. Lanham, MD: Rowman & Littlefield.

Campbell, Angus, Philip E. Converse, Warren E. Miller, and Donald E. Stokes. 1960. *The American Voter.* New York: John Wiley & Sons.

Casselman, Ben. 2017. Stop Saying Trump's Win Had Nothing to do with Economics. *FiveThirtyEight.com*, January 9. https://fivethirtyeight.com/features/stop-saying-trumps-win-had-nothing-to-do-with-economics/.

Ceasar, James W., Andrew E. Busch, and John J. Pitney Jr. 2017. *Defying the Odds: The 2016 Elections and American Politics.* Lanham, MD: Rowman & Littlefield.

Cohen, Marshall, and Jeff Simon. 2016. How Democrats Lost Dubuque, and Middle America. *CNNPolitics,* December 14. https://www.cnn.com/2016/12/14/politics/democrats-lost-dubuque-middle-america/index.html.

Conger, Kimberly H., and Donald Racheter. 2006. Iowa: In the Heart of Bush Country. In *The Values Campaign? The Christian Right and the 2004 Elections,* ed. John C. Green, Mark J. Rozell, and Clyde Wilcox, 128–142. Washington, DC: Georgetown University Press.

Cramer, Katherine J. 2016a. *The Politics of Resentment: Rural Consciousness in Wisconsin and the Rise of Scott Walker.* Chicago: University of Chicago Press.

———. 2016b. For Years, I've Been Watching Anti-Elite Fury Build in Wisconsin. Then Came Trump. *Vox,* November 16. https://www.vox.com/the-big-idea/2016/11/16/13645116/rural-resentment-elites-trump.

David Binder Research (DBR). n.d. Qualitative Research Summary: Riverside and Waterloo, IA. Unpublished Research Report.

Drutman, Lee. 2017. Political Divisions in 2016 and Beyond: Tensions Between and Within the Two Parties. Democracy Fund Voter Study Group, June 2017. https://www.voterstudygroup.org/publications/2016-elections/political-divisions-in-2016-and-beyond.

Enos, Ryan D. 2017. *The Space Between Us: Social Geography and Politics.* New York: Cambridge University Press.

Enten, Harry. 2014. Something Funny Happened in Iowa, and It May Hurt Democrats in 2016. *FiveThirtyEight.com,* November 11. https://fivethirtyeight.com/features/something-funny-happened-in-iowa-and-it-may-hurt-democrats-in-2016/.

———. 2016. It's Not All About Clinton – The Midwest Was Getting Redder Before 2016. *FiveThirtyEight.com,* December 9. https://fivethirtyeight.com/features/its-not-all-about-clinton-the-midwest-was-getting-redder-before-2016/.

Evich, Helena Bottemiller. 2016. Revenge of the Rural Voter. *Politico,* November 13. https://www.politico.com/story/2016/11/hillary-clinton-rural-voters-trump-231266.

Exit Polls. 2012a. Exit Polls: President Full Results. Last Modified December 10, 2012. http://www.cnn.com/election/2012/results/race/president/.

———. 2012b. Exit Polls: Iowa President. Last Modified December 10. http://www.cnn.com/election/2012/results/state/IA/president/.

———. 2016a. Exit Polls: National President. Last Modified November 23. https://www.cnn.com/election/2016/results/exit-polls.

———. 2016b. Exit Polls: Iowa President. Last Modified November 23. https://www.cnn.com/election/2016/results/exit-polls/iowa/president.

Fennelly, Katherine, and Christopher Federico. 2008. Rural Residence as a Determinant of Attitudes Toward US Immigration Policy. *International Migration* 46 (1): 151–190. https://doi.org/10.1111/j.1468-2435.2008.00440.x.

Hardy, Kevin. 2016. The Immigration Divide. *Des Moines Register*, November 1. ProQuest.

Hoffman, Donna R., and Christopher W. Larimer. 2015. Battleground Iowa: Swing State Extraordinaire. In *Presidential Swing States: Why Only Ten Matter*, ed. Stacey Hunter Hecht and David Schultz, 265–289. Lanham, MD: Lexington Books.

Hohmann, James. 2016. Why the GOP Establishment Embraces Trump in Iowa More Than Any Other Battleground. *The Daily 202* (blog), *Washington Post*, August 29. https://www.washingtonpost.com/news/powerpost/paloma/daily-202/2016/08/29/daily-202-why-the-gop-establishment-embraces-trump-in-iowa-more-than-any-other-battleground/57c36df3cd249a6fcdd b9f50/.

Hooghe, Marc, and Ruth Dassonneville. 2018. Explaining the Trump Vote: The Effect of Racist Resentment and Anti-Immigrant Sentiments. *PS: Political Science & Politics* 51 (3): 528–534. https://doi.org/10.1017/S1049096518000367.

Hopkins, Daniel J. 2010. Politicized Places: Explaining Where and When Immigrants Provoke Local Opposition. *American Political Science Review* 104 (1): 40–60. https://doi.org/10.1017/S0003055409990360.

Iowa Secretary of State (IA SOS). 2012. 2012 General Election Canvass Summary. https://sos.iowa.gov/elections/pdf/2012/general/canvsummary.pdf.

———. 2016a. 2016 General Election Canvass Summary. https://sos.iowa.gov/elections/pdf/2016/primary/canvsummary.pdf.

———. 2016b. State of Iowa Voter Registration Totals: County (11/1/2016). https://sos.iowa.gov/elections/pdf/VRStatsArchive/2016/CoNov16.pdf.

Iowa State Data Center (ISDC). n.d. *Urban and Rural Population (100-Percent Data) in Iowa and Its Counties: 1980–2000.* Accessed March 20, 2019. https://www.iowadatacenter.org/datatables/CountyAll/courbanrural19802000.pdf.

Iyengar, Shanto, and Sean J. Westwood. 2015. Fear and Loathing Across Party Lines: New Evidence on Group Polarization. *American Journal of Political Science* 59 (3): 690–707. https://doi.org/10.1111/ajps.12152.

Jones, Robert P. 2016. Donald Trump and the Transformation of White Evangelicals. *Time*, November 19. http://time.com/4577752/donald-trump-transformation-white-evangelicals/.

Kaufmann, Jeff. 2019. Interview by Author. *Des Moines*, February 14.

Larimer, Christopher W., and Donna R. Hoffman. 2018. Iowa: The Religious Right as Sometime Republican Kingmaker. In *God at the Grassroots 2016: The*

Christian Right in American Politics, ed. Mark J. Rozell and Clyde Wilcox, 49–67. Lanham, MD: Rowman & Littlefield.

Lay, J. Celeste. 2012. *A Midwestern Mosaic: Immigration and Political Socialization in Rural America*. Philadelphia: Temple University Press.

Longworth, Richard C. 2016. Disaffected Rust Belt Voters Embraced Trump. They Had No Other Hope. *The Guardian*, November 21. https://www.theguardian.com/commentisfree/2016/nov/21/disaffected-rust-belt-voters-embraced-donald-trump-midwestern-obama.

Malone, Clare. 2016. Clinton Couldn't Win Over White Women. *FiveThirtyEight.com*, November 9. https://fivethirtyeight.com/features/clinton-couldnt-win-over-white-women/.

McElwee, Sean, and Jason McDaniel. 2017. Economic Anxiety Didn't Make People Vote for Trump, Racism Did. *Nation*, May 8. https://www.thenation.com/article/economic-anxiety-didnt-make-people-vote-trump-racism-did/.

Miller, Warren E., and J. Merrill Shanks. 1996. *The New American Voter*. Cambridge, MA: Harvard University Press.

Mutz, Diana C. 2018. Status Threat, Not Economic Hardship, Explains the 2016 Presidential Vote. *Proceedings of the National Academy of Sciences of the United States of America* 115 (19): 1–10. https://doi.org/10.1073/pnas.1718155115.

Noble, Jason. 2016a. Iowa GOP Denounces Trump's Remarks. *Des Moines Register*, October 9. ProQuest.

———. 2016b. In Iowa, Leaders of GOP Lock Arms for Trump. *Des Moines Register*, October 30. ProQuest.

———. 2016c. Down Stretch, Trump Leads. *Des Moines Register*, November 6. ProQuest.

Petroski, William. 2016a. Branstad Defends Trump, Warns of ISIS Threat to Iowans. *Des Moines Register*, October 11. ProQuest.

———. 2016b. Ernst Backs Trump, GOP Ticket. *Des Moines Register*, October 11. ProQuest.

Posner, Sarah. 2017. Amazing Disgrace. *New Republic*, March 20. https://newrepublic.com/article/140961/amazing-disgrace-donald-trump-hijacked-religious-right.

Racheter, Donald P., Lyman A. Kellstedt, and John C. Green. 2003. Iowa: Crucible of the Christian Right. In *The Christian Right in American Politics: Marching to the Millennium*, ed. John C. Green, Mark J. Rozell, and Clyde Wilcox, 121–144. Washington, DC: Georgetown University Press.

Rapoport, Ronald B., and Walter J. Stone. 2017. The Sources of Trump's Support. In *Trumped: The 2016 Election That Broke All the Rules*, ed. Larry J. Sabato, Kyle Kondik, and Geoffrey Skelley, 136–151. Lanham, MD: Rowman & Littlefield.

Reny, Tyler T., Loren Collingwood, and Ali A. Valenzuela. 2019. Vote Switching in the 2016 Election: How Racial and Immigration Attitudes, Not Economics, Explain Shifts in White Voting. *Public Opinion Quarterly* 83 (1): 91–113. https://doi.org/10.1093/poq/nfz011.

Rhoads, James, Dan B. Thomas, and Bruce F. McKeown. 2017. Rationality vs. Rationale Among Trump Voters in 2016: What Were They Thinking? *Operant Subjectivity: The International Journal of Q Methodology* 39 (3/4): 60–80. https://doi.org/10.15133/j.os.2017.012.

Schaffner, Brian F., Matthew MacWilliams, and Tatishe Nteta. 2018. Understanding White Polarization in the 2016 Vote for President: The Sobering Role of Racism and Sexism. *Political Science Quarterly* 133 (1): 9–34. https://doi.org/10.1002/polq.12737.

Sides, John, Michael Tesler, and Lynn Vavreck. 2018. *Identity Crisis: The 2016 Presidential Campaign and the Battle for the Meaning of America.* Princeton, NJ: Princeton University Press.

Silver, Nate. 2016. The Mythology of Trump's 'Working Class' Support. *FiveThirtyEight.com*, May 3. https://fivethirtyeight.com/features/the-mythology-of-trumps-working-class-support/.

———. 2017a. The Real Story of 2016. *FiveThirtyEight.com*, January 19. https://fivethirtyeight.com/features/the-real-story-of-2016/.

———. 2017b. The Electoral College Blind Spot. *FiveThirtyEight.com*, January 23. https://fivethirtyeight.com/features/the-electoral-college-blind-spot/.

Stetzer, Ed, and Andrew MacDonald. 2018. Why Evangelicals Voted Trump: Debunking the 81%. *Christianity Today*, October 18. https://www.christianitytoday.com/ct/2018/october/why-evangelicals-trump-vote-81-percent-2016-election.html.

Stewart, Katherine. 2016. Eighty-One Percent of White Evangelicals Voted for Donald Trump. Why? *Nation*, November 17. https://www.thenation.com/article/eighty-one-percent-of-white-evangelicals-voted-for-donald-trump-why/.

Trende, Sean. 2017. The 'Emerging Democratic Majority' Fails to Emerge. In *Trumped: The 2016 Election That Broke All the Rules*, ed. Larry J. Sabato, Kyle Kondik, and Geoffrey Skelley, 211–226. Lanham, MD: Rowman & Littlefield.

U.S. Census Bureau. 2002a. Profile of Selected Economic Characteristics: 2000. Released September 25, 2002.

———. 2002b. Profile of General Demographic Characteristics: 2000. Released October 23, 2002.

———. 2015. 2010 Census Urban and Rural Classification and Urban Area Criteria. Last Revised February 9, 2015. https://www.census.gov/geo/reference/ua/urban-rural-2010.html.

———. 2017a. ACS Demographic and Housing Estimates: 2012–2016 American Community Survey 5-Year Estimates. Released December 7, 2017.

————. 2017b. Educational Attainment: 2012–2016 American Community Survey 5-Year Estimates. Released December 7, 2017.

————. 2017c. Selected Economic Characteristics: 2012–2016 American Community Survey 5-Year Estimates. Released December 7, 2017.

U.S. Department of Agriculture, Economic Research Service (USDA-ERS). 2013. Rural-Urban Continuum Codes. Released May 10, 2013. https://www.ers.usda.gov/data-products/rural-urban-continuum-codes/.

Wasserman, David. 2017. The One County in America That Voted in a Landslide for Both Trump and Obama. *FiveThirtyEight.com*, November 9. https://fivethirtyeight.com/features/the-one-county-in-america-that-voted-in-a-landslide-for-both-trump-and-obama/.

Williams, Joan C. 2016. What So Many People Don't Get About the U.S. Working Class. *Harvard Business Review*, November 10. https://hbr.org/2016/11/what-so-many-people-dont-get-about-the-u-s-working-class.

Wuthnow, Robert. 2018. *The Left Behind: Decline and Rage in Rural America*. Princeton, NJ: Princeton University Press.

Zitner, Aaron, and Paul Overberg. 2016. Rural Vote Fuels Trump; Clinton Loses Urban Grip. *Wall Street Journal*, November 9. ProQuest.

Zoll, Rachel. 2016. Why Do Evangelicals Prefer Donald Trump to Hillary Clinton. *AP News*, October 11. https://www.apnews.com/8dc1e6a172bc49c2817ca5cb7c463286.

CHAPTER 4

Explaining Vote Choice in 2016: How the Attitudinal Characteristics of Iowans Shaped the Vote for Donald Trump

I definitely think racism and sexism both played a part at both the state and national level, but I'm less clear on how much of a difference it made. Iowans tend to personally be more conservative on questions of immigration, racial justice, and religious tolerance, but also less inclined to force their personal positions on others. Trump's campaign was founded on xenophobic anti-immigration rhetoric, so I'm sure there was some percentage of irregular Iowa voters that responded to that. Exit polls showed that voters approved of many of Clinton's policies but not Clinton herself, and I'm sure sexism played into that, as well.
—*Democratic County Party Official from southeast Iowa*

Abstract In this chapter, I present a discussion of the academic literature oriented toward presidential elections, Iowa elections, and the 2016 election. The literature is used to theoretically develop models of vote choice using individual-level data. The individual-level findings demonstrate that the 2016 election was not driven solely by white, working-class support. Rather, support for Donald Trump was driven by partisanship, attitudes regarding President Obama's performance, and hardline positions on immigration. Additionally, educational attainment did not drive vote switching in 2016 either. Vote switching—casting a vote for Obama or a third-party candidate in 2012 and then for Trump in 2016—was both a function of voters' approval of Obama's performance as president and their attitudes about race.

© The Author(s) 2020
A. D. Green, *From the Iowa Caucuses to the White House*,
Palgrave Studies in US Elections,
https://doi.org/10.1007/978-3-030-22499-8_4

Keywords Presidential performance • Educational attainment
• Partisanship • Immigration • Racial attitudes

Part of Donald Trump's "Make America Great Again" agenda involved significant reform to America's immigration system, a system he called "dysfunctional" in a campaign speech after the Pulse nightclub shooting in Orlando, Florida (Golshan 2016). Trump often talked about the issue of immigration, focusing primarily on what he perceived as a linkage between undocumented migrants and violent crime in the United States. As Lind (2019) recently wrote, "the idea that immigrants are coming to kill you is a persistent motif in his scripted speeches," not only on the campaign trail but also after being elected president. At times, Trump's rhetoric was inflammatory, often stereotyping immigrants—particularly immigrants from Mexico, central America, and the Middle East—as criminals, murderers, rapists, drug mules, and terrorists. Even though Trump's claims ran counter to studies demonstrating that immigrants, both documented and undocumented, commit fewer crimes than native-born Americans (Nowrasteh 2018), he continued to reinforce this narrative in speech after speech, at rally after rally from the time he announced his candidacy at Trump Tower in June 2015 until Election Day in November 2016.

Attitudes about race and how they impact elections in the United States are linked to the immigration narrative from 2016. Research on the impact of racial attitudes on politics and elections reveals that attitudes regarding race impact how Americans view policy issues (e.g., Tesler 2012; Filindra and Kaplan 2016) and candidates (e.g., Piston 2010; Knuckey and Kim 2015; Valentino et al. 2018b). It is certainly plausible that Trump's rhetoric on immigration and nationalism could have served as a cue to prime Iowa voters with more conservative attitudes on race, thus creating a causal pathway between the racial attitudes of voters and support for Trump in the 2016 election, as some national-level research has indicated (e.g., Hooghe and Dassonneville 2018; Setzler and Yanus 2018; Sides et al. 2018; Abramowitz and McCoy 2019; Reny et al. 2019).

For Iowans, were attitudes about immigration and race important predictors of vote choice in 2016, even when controlling for other predictors of vote choice? The epigraph above is a good synopsis of the opinions of Iowa political elites regarding the question. As detailed in Chap. 2, evidence of racism or sexism in the interviews of state political elites and in the survey of county party officials is mixed at best. Some respondents to the survey and several interviewees were definitive in their conclusion that neither racism nor sexism played a role citing Barack Obama's success in Iowa (twice) and the recent election of women to statewide offices: Joni Ernst to the U.S. Senate and Kim Reynolds as Governor. Other participants were definitive in their conclusion that racism or sexism did play a role in explaining 2016. Furthermore, some respondents and interviewees, like the county party official quoted in the epigraph, fell somewhere in between, acknowledging that race and gender may have played a role but were unsure of the effect these elements had on the outcome of the election.

To determine whether immigration and racial attitudes played a role in shaping a preference for Donald Trump in Iowa, statistical models of Trump support were developed to control for other predictors of vote choice, including partisanship, issue preferences, retrospective evaluations, and key demographic characteristics. The models demonstrate that attitudes about immigration, the assessment of President Obama's performance, and partisanship were significant predictors of Iowans voting for Trump in 2016. While racial attitudes were not directly linked to a vote for Trump, they (along with the Obama approval rating and partisanship) were directly linked to Iowa voters who preferred a candidate other than Mitt Romney in 2012 (e.g., Barack Obama or Gary Johnson) and then voted for Trump in 2016.[1]

4.1 Theoretical Development and Data

The primary assumption of the empirical work below is that a voter's decision between candidates is a function of his or her party identification, how the voter assesses characteristics of the candidates, and the voter's attitudinal predispositions about salient issues. Grounded in *The American Voter* (Campbell et al. 1960) and more recent work by Achen and Bartels (2016), it is assumed voters viewed the candidates and the salient issues in 2016 through the lens of their party identification and social identity. For voters, partisanship and social identity should have shaped their assessments of President Obama's job performance; assessments about the relevant characteristics of Donald Trump and Hillary Clinton; the positions they took on the important issues of the campaign; and ultimately the candidate who they voted for. After assessing the relevant literature and the qualitative data described in Chap. 2, I expect support for Donald Trump in Iowa to be a function of partisanship; racial attitudes; assessments of Barack Obama's performance as president and of the economy; and positions on relevant issues such as abortion, guns, and immigration.[2]

The data utilized here is from the Common Content of the 2016 Cooperative Congressional Election Survey (CCES) (Ansolabehere and Schaffner 2017).[3] The CCES is a multi-wave online panel study of 64,600 Americans. Participants were provided the first wave in the months leading up to the November election and were then invited to participate in the second wave of the study in the aftermath of the November election, through mid-December 2016. Of the 64,600 participants, 613 are Iowans. The sample was then limited to white Iowa respondents, leaving 570 cases to analyze. All descriptive findings and analyses are weighted to generalize about the attitudes and behaviors of white Iowa voters during the 2016 election. A description of the CCES item(s) for each predictor assessed is provided below, along with a theoretical rationale for inclusion in the analyses.[4]

I was interested in assessing Iowa voter support for Donald Trump and vote switching in the state in 2016. To do so, two dependent variables were used. First, a dichotomous variable coded 1 for Trump Voters and 0 for all else (i.e., Clinton or a third-party candidate) was used to measure support for Trump in Iowa.[5] Of the valid responses, 51.8% reported voting for Trump and 48.2% reported voting for another candidate, which is close to the actual outcome of the election. A second dependent variable was created to explain vote switching in 2016. For the purposes of this chapter, vote switching is defined as an Iowa voter who cast a 2012 ballot for any candidate other than Mitt Romney and then cast a ballot for Donald Trump in 2016. This variable is also dichotomous and is coded 1 for Iowa voters who switched to Trump. It is coded 0 for all other Iowa voters who self-reported a vote choice for 2012 and 2016. After excluding missing cases, about 9% ($N = 41.6$) of valid cases report voting for Trump in 2016, after either voting for Obama or a third party candidate in 2012.[6]

The relationship between partisanship and presidential vote has been established in the literature. Dating back to *The American Voter* (Campbell et al. 1960), partisans are expected to vote for their party's candidate unless short-term forces in economic performance or the campaign lead them to defect. Thus in 2016, ceteris paribus, one would expect Republicans to support Donald Trump and Democrats to support Hillary Clinton. As discussed in Chap. 3, movement toward what political scientists call "affective" or "negative" partisanship has led voters to assess members of their own party more favorably and to hold negative views of opposing partisans, leading to increased levels of straight-ticket voting (Iyengar and Westwood 2015; Abramowitz and Webster 2016).

Partisanship is included using dummy variables to represent the self-reported party ID of Iowa respondents. CCES participants were asked the standard three-question party identification battery to create a seven-point partisanship measure ranging from "Strong Democrat" to "Strong Republican." "Leaning" Independents, or registered Independents who "lean" toward one of the major political parties, were coded as partisans. It is well-documented that leaning partisans tend to have preferences similar to partisans, and they behave like partisans in elections (e.g., Keith et al. 1992; Magleby et al. 2011; Klar and Krupnikov 2016). In other words, leaning partisans are indeed partisans without the official party affiliation label, and they are thus treated as partisans. Democrats are treated as the reference group when predicting a vote for Trump, so it is expected that Iowa Republicans would be more likely than Iowa Democrats to support Trump.

Predicting the impact of being an Independent, or a "No Party" voter, is a bit more difficult. Once leaning partisans are removed, the partisan cue for explaining vote choice disappears. The literature on Iowa politics offers little guidance on the voting behavior of No Party voters because a comprehensive analysis of No Party voters has not been undertaken by political scientists. The interview and survey data may provide a small cue, however, about how No Party voters behaved in 2016. The consensus among the state political elites interviewed for the project asserted that the driving force behind the switch in No Party support for Obama in 2012 to Trump in 2016 was "change." According to many of the interviews, No Party voters were change voters looking for something different in Washington. This sentiment was echoed by several county party officials in the survey as well. If No Party voters were truly looking for change in 2016, then No Party voters more than likely voted for Trump because he was viewed as the lone outsider candidate who would bring change to Washington, D.C.

Racial attitudes have long been linked to political outcomes in the United States as well. Research in the field has examined not only the role of racial attitudes in candidate choice, but also how racial attitudes shape voter perceptions of public policy. For example, issues such as gun control and healthcare reform have become "racialized" in the modern era. In other words, the policy preferences of individuals are shaped by the racial attitudes the voter holds (Tesler 2012; Filindra and Kaplan 2016). Tesler (2012, 691) notes some policies, such as affirmative action, have "clear-cut racial content," which makes the connection between the policy and racial attitudes very clear. However, other policies lacking such racial content can also be racialized. Filindra and Kaplan believe racialization of the gun control issue is grounded in the origins of gun control policies during the Civil Rights Movement. Meanwhile, Tesler argues that the racialization of healthcare reform is grounded in President Obama becoming the champion of efforts to reform the healthcare system.

While research on the role of racial attitudes dates back decades, the last decade has seen research primarily focused on the impact of racial attitudes on the election and re-election of Barack Obama, the country's first black president. For example, Piston (2010) found that holding negative stereotypes about blacks (e.g., lazy, unintelligent) was related to diminished support among white voters for Barack Obama in 2008. The relationship between stereotypes and vote choice was nuanced by party identification. Specifically, the effect of stereotypes had little effect on Republican support for Obama but led to diminished support among Democrats. It had an even larger negative impact on the probability of Independents voting for Obama. Research on Obama's 2012 re-election also demonstrates that white voters holding negative stereotypes and racially resentful attitudes were less likely to support Obama. Knuckey and Kim (2015), however, disaggregate the electorate by geographic region, comparing voters in the south to nonsouthern voters. They found substantial differences by region. Whereas the likelihood of southern, white voters voting for Obama was shaped by racial resentment alone, nonsouthern voters were less likely to vote for Obama if they held racially resentful attitudes and negative stereotypes about African Americans. They also found the relationship was shaped by party ID. Consistent with Piston's findings, racial attitudes had the largest effect on the voting patterns of Independent voters.

Why might we expect that the racial attitudes of Iowa voters played a role in the election of Donald Trump, a state won by Barack Obama on two separate occasions? First, there is evidence of racial resentment in rural America oriented toward hard work. Residents who were perceived as lazy, fiscally irresponsible, or expecting handouts for little work are often identified as "riff-raff." Wuthnow (2018, 152–153) notes, "riff-raff could be anybody–white Anglo, Hispanic, or African American–but in communities where there were any African Americans, they were the implied referent." In rural America, racial attitudes can manifest themselves in resentment toward urban areas with larger populations of racial and ethnic minorities. It is important to note, however, that racial attitudes are not the sole cause of rural resentment (Cramer 2016).

Second, research on the 2016 election demonstrates that racial attitudes mattered. A popular narrative in the aftermath of 2016, as described in Chaps. 2 and 3, purported that the education gap and economic anxiety, not racism or sexism, were the drivers of Trump's support in 2016. However, this narrative has been widely dismissed through the work of political scientists using experimental methods and national-level data. A recent experimental investigation revealed that racially charged political messaging is accepted among voters and predicts not only policy support but also candidate support (Valentino et al. 2018b). Statistical models of vote choice have shown support for Trump is driven in part by racial attitudes as well. In many studies, the effect of educational attainment or economic anxiety was greatly diminished (or non-existent) once racial attitudes were introduced (e.g., McElwee and McDaniel 2017; Schaffner et al. 2018; Setzler and Yanus 2018; Sides et al. 2018; Abramowitz and McCoy 2019). Racial attitudes were also a significant predictor in vote switching to Trump in 2016 vis-à-vis economic explanations or demographic change (Reny et al. 2019).

Third, it would not be surprising to find higher levels of animosity toward racial and ethnic minorities (and higher levels of economic anxiety) in Iowa because of the state's small proportion of college educated individuals. Research shows that educational attainment is related to perceptions of race and immigration. Abramowitz and McCoy's (2019) study of the 2016 election finds that 31% of college-educated voters score high on measures of racial resentment. For non-college-educated voters, the figure was 50%. The difference for anti-immigration views was 23% (27% for college educated versus 50% for non-college educated). Additionally, McElwee and McDaniel (2017) found the best predictors of economic anxiety among white voters to include attitudes regarding immigrants and African Americans. Hence, it is understandable why the impact of educational attainment and economic anxiety on support for Trump would diminish when racial attitudes are introduced.

Then, why would Iowa voters support Obama twice, a black candidate for president, if they held racially conservative views? The answer lies in the activation of political preferences during campaigns. Campaigns serve an important purpose for voters by providing information that has the effect of activating certain political predispositions (Bartels 1988). The now-activated predispositions can then shape how voters view the candidates and, ultimately, the choice a voter makes. Sides et al. (2018) argue that this phenomenon is exactly what happened in 2016. Against the backdrop of a partisan realignment along racial lines, predispositions oriented toward identity were activated by the campaigns of both Trump and Hillary Clinton, making those predispositions relevant in making a choice on Election Day. Identity-based attitudes were not nearly as relevant in 2008 and 2012 because they were not activated by the candidates. So, voters with unfavorable attitudes about African Americans or immigrants were willing to vote for a black candidate for president. In 2016 when those preferences were activated, they rejected the candidate who was campaigning for Obama's third term.

The CCES battery of questions regarding race and racism was used to assess the impact of racial attitudes on Trump support in Iowa. The first two questions in the battery assess whether the voter is aware or acknowledges that racism exists in the United States, which are elements of what Neville et al. (2000) call "color-blind racial attitudes." The third item in the battery assesses whether the respondent cares that racism exists in America or whether they empathize with the victims of racism (Schaffner et al. 2018). To assess views regarding modern racism, respondents were asked to identify their level of agreement to the following statements: "White people in the U.S. have certain advantages because of the color of their skin"; "Racial problems in the U.S. are rare, isolated situations"; and "I am angry that racism exists" (Ansolabehere and Schaffner 2017). An additive index of the measures was created ($\alpha = 0.70$) and then scaled to range from "most acknowledging" of racism (0) to "most denying" of racism (1). If racial attitudes were an important predictor of support for Donald Trump in the state, the expectation becomes that the measure will be positively associated with support for Trump.[7]

As discussed in Chap. 2, presidential candidates are often evaluated "retrospectively," or backward-looking (Key 1966). Voters will often make decisions in elections based upon their perception of the president's performance, thus a positive presidential performance rating can lead the voter to choose an incumbent (or the incumbent party's candidate) over a challenger (Fiorina 1981). Conversely, voters who perceive the president's performance as being poor will often vote for change in the form of a challenger. Additionally, voters use readily available information about the state of the national economy (i.e., "sociotropic" evaluations) or their own personal financial condition (i.e., "pocketbook" evaluations) to assess the performance of presidents and render a judgment in a specific election (Kinder and Kiewiet 1981). While sociotropic assessments require voters to understand macroeconomic indicators and what they mean, pocketbook assessments for the average voter involve information readily available to them. A voter may not know what the unemployment or inflation rate are; but, in assessing their personal financial condition, voters only need to look toward their personal savings, take home pay, or disposable income to determine where they stand financially. In what Popkin (1994, 22) calls the "by-product theory of political information," voters then utilize information collected through their daily experiences to make political decisions, including voting decisions. If the information regarding personal financial condition is positive, then voters reward the incumbent or incumbent party's candidate with another term (Hibbs 1987).

Two retrospective assessments are included in the modeling of Trump support. Multiple interviewees and respondents to the survey of county party officials indicated that 2016 was a "change" election. In other words, voters were not happy with the performance of the federal government and the direction of the country, so they went to the polls to vote for a candidate who would bring change to Washington, D.C. If 2016 was indeed a change election, one would assume that President Obama's presidential approval rating would then be associated with vote choice. Exit polling certainly showed that Iowa voters who disapproved of Obama's performance were very likely to vote for Trump. In fact, nearly 90% of Iowa voters who disapproved of Obama's performance did report voting for Trump (Exit Polls 2016). The CCES asked respondents to provide their approval rating for a series of elected officials and political institutions. The measure of Obama's performance is a recoded measure which collapses "strongly approve" and "somewhat approve" into one approval category coded 0 while "strongly disapprove" and "somewhat disapprove" are collapsed into one disapproval category coded 1. The expectation is that disapproval of Obama's performance would be positively associated with support for Trump in Iowa.

The economy was certainly salient to Iowa voters in 2016. According to exit polls, 54% of Iowa voters cited the economy as the "most important issue facing the country" (Exit Polls 2016). County party officials also identified the economy as a salient issue to Trump and Clinton voters. In the open-ended question which asked respondents to identify the three most important issues to Trump and Clinton voters, the economy was the second-most-cited issue for both cohorts of voters. Additionally, the average

score for the economy on the closed-ended item regarding issue importance, which ranged from "not very important (1) to "very important" (5),
was 4.3 for Trump voters and 4.05 for Clinton voters. The question was
whether to use the sociotropic or the pocketbook CCES item. In the end,
the pocketbook item was included in the modeling. There were several
reasons for this decision. First, the inclusion of both measures could create
multicollinearity issues in the modeling, as the correlation between the
sociotropic and pocketbook measures is 0.425. Second, if economic anxiety
was a driver of Trump support, the measure of personal financial condition
is the best proxy since it asks the respondent to assess any change in their
household income over the prior four years. It is reasonable to assume that
respondents who indicated their household income had gone down over
the previous four years would be more economically anxious. Additionally,
household income is going to be sensitive to job loss, the impacts of benefit
costs on take-home pay, and wage growth (or loss). Third, the sociotropic
measure is significantly influenced by partisanship (e.g., Bartels 2002). The
measures in the CCES are no different. In fact, the influence of party ID on
the sociotropic measure was much stronger than it was on the pocketbook
measure. Finally, research shows that perceptions of the national economy
can be shaped by presidential campaigns, even when objective indicators of
economic performance run counter to mass perception (Hetherington
1996). Iowans were pessimistic about the condition of the national economy on Election Day: 63% of voters polled said the national economy was
either "not good" or "poor" (Exit Polls 2016). This observation runs
counter to what macroeconomic indicators were revealing: Namely, the
economy was improving during the latter portion of the Obama administration (Lewis 2017), so perceptions could have been shaped by the fact
that the sitting president was a Democrat or by campaign rhetoric from the
candidates (or both).

The pocketbook measure was created from responses to the question
"Over the past FOUR YEARS, has your household's income ...?"
(Ansolabehere and Schaffner 2017). The item is a five-point scale ranging
from "Increased a lot" (1) to "Decreased a lot" (5). The measure was
scaled to range from 0 to 1. The expectation proffers that as the perception of personal financial condition decreases, support for Trump in Iowa
should increase.

Salient issues of the campaign should also impact the decision of voters.
Within the context of the *American Voter* model (Campbell et al. 1960;
Miller and Shanks 1996), issue positions are shaped by partisan identifica-

tion and are short-term electoral factors that shape vote choice. As a result, the importance of issues in explaining vote choice will vary from election to election, based upon the ability of candidates to activate voter predispositions about policy. The information provided by candidates to voters not only activates long-standing political predispositions but also impacts how voters evaluate candidates in the race. With more political information, voters can more accurately assess the issue positions of the candidates vis-à-vis their own issue positions to make a choice (Bartels 1988). Additionally, as voters typically possess relatively low levels of political information about issue positions and how policymaking works, they are reliant on the candidates to provide them with information on the issues, how the office they are seeking influences policy, and the differences between the candidates on salient issues (Popkin 1994). Voters are utility maximizers and thus need to understand what policy positions the candidates hold and how the office they are seeking will shape issue-based campaign promises into real-life policy outcomes.

Data from exits polls and from the survey of county party officials was used to identify major campaign issues that could be related to support for Donald Trump in Iowa. According to exit polls, the top four most important issues, as identified by Iowa voters, were the economy (54%), terrorism (18%), immigration (12%), and foreign policy (12%) (Exit Polls 2016). For the open-ended question regarding the most important issue to Trump voters; immigration, the economy, and abortion were the only issues to receive double-digit mentions from county party officials (see Fig. 3.1 in Chap. 3). On the closed-ended item of issue importance scaled from "not very important" (1) to "very important" (5), immigration ranked second with an average score of 4.57. The economy was ranked third with an average score of 4.3, while abortion ranked fourth ($\mu = 4.27$) and terrorism was fifth ($\mu = 3.98$). The top-ranked issue, however, was gun rights, with an average score of 4.7 on a five-point scale. Foreign policy had an average score of 2.94 and fell near the middle of all issues probed. As a result, the models include indices for gun rights, immigration, and abortion based upon the saliency of the issues and availability of data in the CCES to assess their importance.[8]

The gun rights measure is an additive index of the respondent's position on gun regulations and restrictions. Respondents were asked whether they supported four gun-related policy options: "Background checks for all sales including at gun shows and over the Internet," "Prohibit state and local governments from publishing the names and addresses of all gun owners," "Ban assault rifles," and "Make it easier for people to obtain concealed-carry permit" (Ansolabehere and Schaffner 2017). Two of the items were recoded prior to creating the additive index to make the support/oppose options consistent across all four items. The items were then added together ($\alpha = 0.66$) and scaled to range from more restrictions (0) to less restrictions (1). Since Donald Trump made his support for 2nd Amendment rights well known on the campaign trail, the gun rights measure should be positively associated with Trump support.

The immigration measure is an additive index of the respondent's position on immigration policy. Respondents were asked whether they thought that the federal government should: "Grant legal status to all illegal immigrants who have held jobs and paid taxes for at least three years, and had not been convicted of any felony crimes"; "Increase the number of border patrols on the U.S.-Mexican border"; "Grant legal status to people who were brought to the US illegally as children, but who have graduated from a U.S. high school"; and "Identify and deport illegal immigrants" (Ansolabehere and Schaffner 2017). Two of the items were recoded prior to creating the additive index to make the options consistent across all four items. The items were then added together ($\alpha = 0.76$) and scaled to range from more pro-immigration (0) to more hardline on immigration (1). As discussed above, Trump made issues of immigration central to his campaign in 2016. Therefore, it is expected that the immigration measure will be positively associated with Trump support.[9]

The abortion measure is also an additive index of the respondent's position on abortion. Respondents were asked if they supported any of the following six policy options: "Always allow a woman to obtain an abortion as a matter of choice," "Permit abortion only in the case of rape, incest or when the woman's life is in danger," "Prohibit all abortions after the 20th week of pregnancy," "Allow employers to decline coverage of abortions in insurance plans," "Prohibit the expenditure of funds authorized or appropriated by federal law for any abortion," and "Make abortions illegal in all circumstances" (Ansolabehere and Schaffner 2017). Two of the items were recoded prior to the additive index's creation to make the options consistent across all six items. The items were then added together ($\alpha = 0.59$) and scaled to range from a very liberal position on abortion (0) to a very conservative position on abortion (1). Throughout the campaign, Trump made his support for ending abortion and the appointment of pro-life justices to the bench a priority. As a result, it is expected that the abortion measure will be positively associated with Trump support.

A series of control variables were also introduced into the modeling to account for important demographic and political characteristics. The demographic controls include the respondent's educational attainment (1 = College Degree, 0 = No College Degree), whether the respondent is an evangelical Christian (1 = Yes, 0 = No), and whether the respondent is male (1 = Yes, 0 = No). A measure of when the respondent voted was also included in the modeling to potentially control for when the voter made his or her presidential vote choice, as there is some evidence which indicates that late deciding voters supported Trump more so than Clinton (McKee et al. 2019).

4.2   Predicting Support for Trump Among White Voters in Iowa

There is preliminary support for the study predictions at the bivariate level. All seven predictors have a statistically significant relationship with vote choice at the bivariate level. As expected, Iowans who disapproved of President Obama's performance were nearly six times more likely to support Trump ($\chi^2 = 273.5$, $p < 0.001$). Republican voters in Iowa were nearly two times as likely as No Party voters and more than seven times as likely as Democrats to support Trump ($\chi^2 = 247.9$, $p < 0.001$). Additionally, there are significant mean differences on the pocketbook assessment, issue scales, and racial attitudes index for Trump versus non-Trump voters (Fig. 4.1).[10] The mean differences reveal that Trump voters were much more pessimistic about their personal financial condition; held much more conservative positions on gun rights, abortion, and immigration policy; and, on average, were more likely to deny or be less empathetic about racism. Of note here is the magnitude of the mean difference for the immigration predictor. The average score on the immigration measure for non-Trump voters (i.e., voted for Hillary Clinton or a third-party candidate) was 0.34. The average score for Trump voters was more than twice the size at 0.78 ($t = -12.36$, $p < 0.001$) on a measure which ranges from 0 to 1.

Before moving on to the multivariate analysis, it is important to note several of the study predictors vary by educational attainment. In the county-level modeling presented in Chap. 3, the educational attainment of white Iowans was a significant predictor of support for Trump, Trump's overperformance of Romney, and whether the county pivoted from Obama in 2012 to Trump in 2016. In the CCES data, 53.6% of white, working-class Iowans voted for Trump, while 46.2% of white Iowans with a college

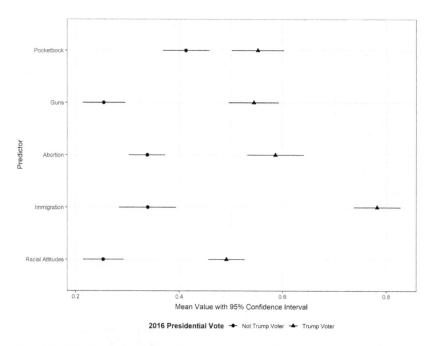

Fig. 4.1 Bivariate relationships between study predictors and a vote for Donald Trump in 2016. Source: 2016 CCES Common Content

degree voted for Trump. The 7.4% difference is not statistically significant ($\chi^2 = 1.99$, $p = 0.2$), however, which is the first clue that something else was driving Trump support in Iowa. As the literature indicates, attitudinal predispositions can vary based upon educational attainment, particularly on matters of race and economic opportunity (Abramowitz and McCoy 2019). Thus, if there are differences in the attitudinal predispositions of white Iowa voters by educational attainment, it could begin to explain the education gap seen in the county-level analyses in the preceding chapter. In other words, if attitudes vary by educational attainment, then introducing the attitudinal predispositions into a model of vote choice should cause educational attainment to fall out of the model altogether.

There are, in fact, differences across the study predictors by educational attainment, but these differences are unique only to the measures of racial attitudes, immigration policy, and personal financial condition. While white, working-class voters were less likely to disapprove of President

Obama's performance (52.5% versus 53.6%), the difference is so small that it is not statistically significant. The finding for the gun rights and abortion measures is identical. White Iowans who have college degrees had slightly lower scores on both measures than those non-college-educated whites, but the differences were not statistically significant either. There were statistically significant differences on the racial attitudes scale, immigration policy index, and pocketbook measure. On the racial attitudes measure, the mean difference between those with a college degree and those without is 0.06 (0.32 versus 0.38, t = 2.23, p = 0.027). On the immigration measure, the mean difference is 0.10 (0.48 versus 0.58, t = 2.37, p = 0.018). And on the pocketbook assessment, the mean difference was 0.09 (0.43 versus 0.50, t = 2.16, p = 0.031). On average, white, working-class voters held more racially conservative attitudes and were more pessimistic about their personal financial condition than those with college degrees.

The results of the multivariate modeling are presented in Table 4.1. Three separate models are presented in the table. The left two columns present the results for the full model of white Iowa voters. Two additional models are presented, disaggregated by educational attainment. The model in the middle two columns presents the results for a model of white, working-class voters. The results for white, college-educated voters are shown in the right two columns. Since logistic regression coefficients are not as easily interpreted as linear regression coefficients, the change in the predicted probability for each significant predictor is provided in the table as well.

For the full model, 11 of the 12 predictors are in the expected direction and three of the predictors are statistically significant. The model reveals that pocketbook assessments, attitudes regarding gun rights and abortion, and identifying as a No Party voter have no independent effect on whether the respondent voted for Donald Trump when controlling for the other predictors in the model. One control, "Election Day Voter," was marginally significant (p = 0.051), suggesting that late-to-decide white voters in Iowa may have broken for Trump consistent with recent research (McKee et al. 2019).

The three significant predictors suggest support for Trump among white Iowa voters was driven by being a Republican, disapproval of President Obama's performance, and holding more hardline views on immigration. Specifically, the results reveal that Republicans had a probability of 0.702 of voting for Trump, compared to a probability of

Table 4.1 Predicting support for Donald Trump among white Iowa voters, 2016

Predictor	All voters		Voters without college degree		Voters with college degree	
	Coefficient	Probability	Coefficient	Probability	Coefficient	Probability
Obama disapproval	2.169***	0.491	2.359***	0.530	0.548	–
Pocketbook	0.958	–	0.551	–	3.136[a]	–
Gun rights	0.868	–	0.745	–	1.979	–
Abortion	0.879	–	1.570	–	0.257	–
Immigration	1.854**	0.428	1.556*	0.370	3.248**	0.658
Racial attitudes	1.172	–	0.591	–	3.292	–
No Party voter	−0.199	–	−0.083	–	0.568	–
Republican voter	1.538**	0.366	1.767**	0.410	1.928	–
Evangelical	0.683	–	1.030[a]	–	−1.429	–
College degree	−0.574	–	–	–	–	–
Male	0.119	–	0.304	–	−1.151	–
Election Day voter	0.745[a]	–	0.919[a]	–	0.711	–
Intercept	−5.094***	–	−5.253***	–	−6.255***	–
$N =$	483		315		168	
$\chi^2 =$	397.037***		264.645***		153.967***	
McFadden's $R^2 =$	0.574		0.570		0.657	

Notes: Coefficients are weighted logistic regression coefficients; the probability column for each model displays the change in the predicted probability of a vote for Trump when moving from 0 to 1 on the predictor while holding the remaining predictors at their mean values. Predicted probabilities were only calculated for the significant predictors in each model; modeled using svyglm (family = quasibinomial, link function = logit) function in R
[a]$p < 0.1$, *$p < 0.05$, **$p < 0.01$, ***$p < 0.001$

0.293 for No Party voters and 0.336 for Democrats. Obama's approval rating also mattered to white Iowa voters. For voters who approved of Obama's performance, the probability of voting for Trump was 0.219. For voters who disapproved of Obama's performance, the probability increased by over 200% to a 71% chance of voting for Trump. Attitudes about immigration also mattered in 2016. The likelihood of voting for

Trump increased nearly twofold, from 0.240 for those who hold the most pro-immigration attitudes to almost a seven in ten chance for voters holding the most hardline positions on immigration.

Furthermore, party identification appears to be mediating the relationship between voting for Trump and immigration attitudes, as well as between Trump support and Obama approval. Figure 4.2 shows the predicted probabilities of voting for Trump by immigration attitudes, disaggregated by party ID. Two things stand out. First, as one moves from left to right on immigration attitudes, the probability of voting for Trump increases, regardless of whether the respondent is a Democrat, a No Party voter, or a Republican. Second, there is an additive effect associated with

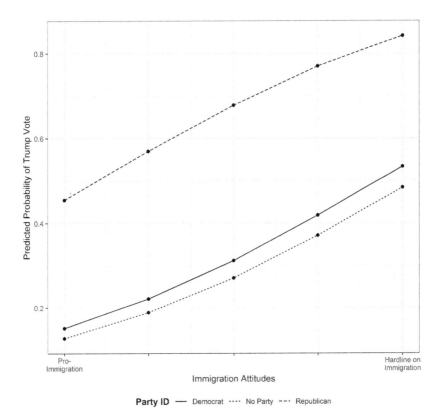

Fig. 4.2 Likelihood of voting for Donald Trump in 2016 by attitudes regarding immigration and party identification. Source: 2016 CCES Common Content

being a Republican. There is clearly very little difference between Democrats and No Party voters in the figure. Both cohorts of voters were more likely to vote for Trump as immigration attitudes became more restrictive, and the total effect of immigration attitudes on voting for Trump was approximately a 37% increase in the likelihood of voting for Trump. The difference between Democratic voters and Republican voters is sizable. At the most pro-immigration position, Republicans had a 45% chance of voting for Trump. At the most hardline, the likelihood was more than eight in ten. There is a similar additive effect present for the association between Obama approval and voting for Trump as well. Both No Party voters and Democrats were more likely to vote for Trump if they disapproved of Obama's performance. Furthermore, loading on the disapprove category led to a probability of voting for Trump of 0.533 for No Party voters and 0.582 for Democrats. For Republicans, there was an 86.6% chance of voting for Trump if the voter disapproved of Obama's performance.

The disaggregated models do reveal differences between white, working-class voters and college-educated whites in Iowa. In the middle two columns of Table 4.1 lies the model for white, working-class voters. Again, 11 of the 12 predictors are in the expected direction. The only predictor with an incorrect sign is the dummy variable for No Party voters. Three of the predictors are statistically significant and two are marginally significant. The two marginally significant predictors included being an evangelical Christian ($p = 0.056$) and being an Election Day voter ($p = 0.067$), suggesting white, working-class voters who are evangelical Christians and Election Day voters may have been more likely to cast a vote for Trump in 2016. A vote for Trump from white, working-class voters was associated with disapproval of President Obama's performance, hardline positions on immigration, and being a Republican. The probability of a Trump vote if the voter disapproved of Obama was 0.761 compared to those who approved of Obama's performance, whose probability was 0.231. This result could suggest support for the "change" narrative heard during the interviews of state political elites and survey responses from county party officials discussed in Chap. 2. Those holding hardline positions on immigration were also more likely to vote for Trump. In fact, white, working-class voters who held the most pro-immigration positions had a 30.7% chance of voting for Trump. Those with hardline positions on immigration had a 67.7% chance. Finally, party ID played a role in explaining the votes of white, working-class voters as well. White, working-class

Republicans had a 75.8% chance of voting for Trump when controlling for the other variables in the model. Identifying as a Republican also amplified the effect of both immigration attitudes and Obama approval on vote choice, with white, working-class Republican voters having a higher likelihood of voting for Trump across all values of both measures.

Significant predictors in the working-class whites model, including Obama approval and identifying as a Republican, were not significant in the college-educated whites model. For college-educated whites (right two columns in Table 4.1), only one predictor was statistically significant: Immigration attitudes. What this finding reveals is that immigration attitudes were not simply a factor for white, working-class voters, but also for white voters with college degrees. In fact, the coefficient for immigration attitudes in the college-educated whites model is double that of the white, working-class voters model. Substantively, for college-educated whites with the most pro-immigration positions, there was a 12% chance of voting for Trump. At the most hardline position, the likelihood increased more than sixfold to 77.8%. The only other variable that nears statistical significance in the model was the pocketbook assessment measure which was positively associated with voting for Trump. The positive coefficient demonstrates that college-educated whites who were pessimistic about their personal financial condition may have been more likely to vote for Trump. It could also suggest support for the "change" narrative. If college-educated voters, voters with far more economic opportunity on average than non-college-educated whites, were pessimistic about their personal financial condition, it could be plausible they went to the polls to vote for a change in leadership in Washington.

The racial attitudes measure fails to reach statistical significance in any of the models displayed in Table 4.1. The coefficients are in the predicted direction in all three models, but the p-values for the coefficients are too large to draw the conclusion that racial attitudes had a *direct* effect on a vote for Donald Trump. However, it is certainly plausible that racial attitudes had an *indirect* effect on vote choice, primarily through the Obama approval and immigration measures, which were significant predictors. Not surprisingly, racial attitudes were associated with approval for President Obama's performance and with attitudes regarding immigration. The mean difference on the racial attitudes measure between Obama approvers ($\mu = 0.24$) and disapprovers ($\mu = 0.48$) is significant ($t = -9.50$, $p < 0.001$). The correlation coefficient for the association between racial attitudes and immigration attitudes is 0.493, which is a robust association.

Therefore, it is certainly possible the impact of conservative racial attitudes was felt indirectly through other measures in the model, even though direct effects are not present.

4.3   Predicting the Likelihood of Being an Iowa Trump Switcher

Vote switching was a significant factor in the 2016 election. As was discussed in Chap. 3, Trump overperformed Mitt Romney by significant margins in several Iowa counties around the state, signifying that many Iowans switched their votes from Barack Obama in 2012 to Donald Trump in 2016. To predict the likelihood of a voter being a "Trump Switcher," a logistic regression model was run with a modified set of the predictors discussed previously. The issue measures for gun rights and abortion were dropped from the model. Theoretically, those holding conservative positions on both guns and abortion should have been more likely to vote Romney in 2012; therefore, they would not be considered Trump Switchers in the model.[11] As a result, the measures were dropped. Second, the order of categories for the party identification variable was flipped so that Republicans were the reference group. Theoretically, Republicans should have a lower likelihood of vote switching because about 90% of Republicans in 2012 voted for Romney and would not be considered vote switchers in 2016 if they voted for Trump. So, the model includes dummy variables for No Party and Democratic voters, with the expectation being that both would be positively related to vote switching to Trump.[12]

The results of the vote switching model are presented in Table 4.2. Nine of the ten predictors are in the anticipated direction. The only predictor to have the incorrect sign is the immigration measure. Due to Trump's campaign narrative regarding immigration, the expectation was that white Iowa voters who held hardline positions on immigration may have been more likely to vote switch to Trump as a result. However, the coefficient was not statistically significant, indicating that immigration attitudes did not have an independent effect on the likelihood of switching from Obama or a third-party candidate in 2012 to Trump in 2016. Coupled with the strong effect of immigration attitudes on support for Trump found in Table 4.1, this finding suggests that respondents with hardline immigration views were probably Romney voters in 2012 and then Trump voters in 2016.

Table 4.2 Predicting the likelihood of vote switching to Trump, 2016

Predictor	Coefficient	SE	Probability
Obama disapproval	1.950*	0.871	0.103
Pocketbook	0.569	1.262	–
Immigration	−0.601	0.906	–
Racial attitudes	2.619*	1.208	0.206
No Party voter	1.400[a]	0.730	–
Democratic voter	2.942**	0.945	0.190
Evangelical	−0.366	0.585	–
College degree	−0.091	0.597	–
Male	−1.005[a]	0.607	–
Election Day voter	0.661	0.599	–
Intercept	−6.029***	1.675	–
N =	456		
χ^2 =	48.867***		
McFadden's R^2 =	0.196		

Notes: Coefficients are weighted logistic regression coefficients; The probability column displays the change in the predicted probability of a vote for Trump when moving from 0 to 1 on the predictor while holding the remaining predictors at their mean values. Predicted probabilities were only calculated for the significant predictors in each model; Modeled using svyglm (family = quasibinomial, link function = logit) function in R
[a]$p < 0.1$, *$p < 0.05$, **$p < 0.01$, ***$p < 0.001$

Overall, the significant predictors reveal that vote switching to Trump was driven by being a Democrat, Obama disapproval, and having conservative attitudes regarding race. The likelihood of vote switching was shaped by the party ID of the voter. Republican voters, as expected, only had a 1.3% chance of switching. The likelihood of No Party voters switching was slightly higher at 5.2%. For Democrats, however, the likelihood was 20.3%, a significant difference from the predicted likelihood of switching for Republicans. Additionally, presidential approval mattered. The positive coefficient indicates that respondents who disapproved of President Obama's performance were more likely to switch their vote to Trump in 2016. Substantively, those white Iowa voters who approved of Obama's performance only had a 1.9% chance of switching, while those who disapproved had a 12.2% chance. Even more striking is the impact of presidential approval on the likelihood of vote switching by party identification. For white Iowa Republicans approving of Obama's performance, the likelihood of switching was almost 0 (0.5%). The likelihood of switching only increased to 3.2% for Republicans who disapproved of his performance ($\Delta = 2.7\%$). The effect was much larger for white No Party voters and even larger for Iowa Democrats. The change in likelihood of vote switching from approval of Obama to disapproval of Obama was 10% for No Party voters (1.9% to 11.9%) and 30.4% for Democrats (8.3% to 38.7%). These findings suggest the "2016 election was a change election" narrative might have some validity, at least with a certain subset of voters who were not thrilled with the performance of President Obama. It certainly provides some evidence to support the "change election" theme borne out of the interview and survey data analyzed in Chap. 2, particularly for No Party voters who may have supported Trump in 2016 after supporting Obama in 2008. What were these voters looking for in both elections? Change.

Unlike in the model of Trump support, the racial attitudes measure is both positive and significant in the Trump vote switching model, consistent with recent research on vote switching in the 2016 election (e.g., Schaffner et al. 2018; Reny et al. 2019). For white Iowa voters with the most liberal attitudes on the modern racism measure, the likelihood of switching to Trump was 2.1%. However, the likelihood of switching when moving from the most liberal attitudes to the most conservative attitudes is ten times larger (22.7%). The relationship between racial attitudes and vote switching is also shaped by party identification. Figure 4.3 shows the effect of racial attitudes on the likelihood of vote switching by party ID. Note the difference in the slope of the lines representing the effect of racial attitudes on vote switching for Republicans, No Party voters, and Democrats. While the slope of the line for white Iowa Republicans is positive, the increased likelihood of vote switching in 2016 is minimal, moving from 0.5% for those Republicans with the most racially liberal attitudes to 6.6% for those with the most racially conservative attitudes. The change in likelihood is far greater for No Party voters at 20.2% (2.0% to 22.2%) and even greater for Democrats at 48.3% (8.9% to 57.2%). The findings in Fig. 4.3 are consistent with previous research on the effect of racial stereotypes on presidential vote choice and how party ID mediates the relationship (Piston 2010; Knuckey and Kim 2015).

4.4   Conclusion

Ultimately, what do the results tell us about the voting behavior of white Iowa voters in the 2016 election? First, there is evidence that 2016 was about "change" for some voters. White Iowa voters who disapproved of President Obama's performance were not only more likely to support

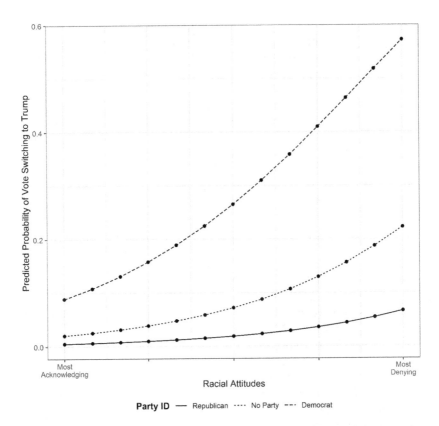

Fig. 4.3 Likelihood of vote switching to Donald Trump in 2016 by attitudes regarding race and party identification. Source: 2016 CCES Common Content

Trump in 2016, many were also more likely to support Trump in 2016 after supporting Obama in 2012 and maybe even in 2008. The modeling indicates the desired change was not about white, working-class voters who were pessimistic about their personal financial condition. This finding refutes a popular narrative about what drove outcomes in 2016. We cannot definitively determine from the modeling what drove the longing for change, but the classic retrospective evaluation is nonetheless indicative of a desire for change. Second, partisanship matters. Not only was partisanship a strong predictor of Trump support in 2016, but it also mediated the relationship between several key predictors and vote choice, including presidential approval, immigration attitudes, and racial attitudes. As we continue into this new era of negative or affective partisanship, it will be even more important to understand how both a voter's party ID and his or her attitudinal predispositions shape vote choice.

Third, predispositions about immigration were important in Iowa as well. Immigration attitudes were a significant predictor of Trump support, which is not surprising considering immigration was the focal point of Trump's 2016 campaign from beginning to end. Additionally, immigration was identified as an important issue in exit polling and by both state and county political elites. Attitudes about immigration were not a predictor of vote switching, however. This fact can most likely be attributed to white Iowa voters with hardline immigration views who supported Romney over Obama in 2012. It is important to note that immigration attitudes were a significant predictor of Trump support, even when controlling for other factors such as Obama approval, salient issues like gun rights and abortion (identified by Iowans as important in 2016), and key demographic and political controls.

What can we conclude about the racial attitudes measure? The modeling demonstrated that racial attitudes were a key driver of vote switching in 2016, particularly for No Party voters and Democratic voters. Does it mean that all Trump supporters are racists? No. Does it mean that some Trump supporters are racists? Maybe. It really tells us two things. First, those who switched their vote from Barack Obama or a third-party candidate in 2012 to Trump in 2016 had higher scores on the modern racism scale. In other words, on average, Trump Switchers were more likely to deny that racism exists or even care that racism exists. Second, among a series of reasons why voters chose Trump, racial attitudes played a role. Racial attitudes certainly played a direct role in vote switching, but also indirectly shaped support for Trump through attitudes regarding President Obama's performance and on immigration issues.

NOTES

1. The epigraph at the beginning of this chapter discusses the likelihood of sexism impacting the decisions of Iowa voters as well. There is certainly a theoretical reason to believe that sexism could have played a role in shaping attitudes toward Hillary Clinton and vote choice in 2016 in Iowa. There is evidence from studies of the U.S. population linking sexism and attitudes regarding Clinton (e.g., McThomas and Tesler 2016) and sexism and vote choice in 2016 (e.g., Setzler and Yanus 2018; Valentino et al.

2018a). A dataset with a large sample of Iowa voters that contained a modern sexism battery was not available to the author. A modern sexism battery is available in the VOTER Survey, but the Iowa subset of the overall sample is 82 cases when accounting for missing data (DFVSG 2017). A basic logistic regression model shows that the modern sexism index ($\alpha = 0.78$) is not a statistically significant predictor of a vote for Trump for white voters in Iowa when controlling for party identification, educational attainment, and gender of the voter. Nor was the modern sexism index a statistically significant predictor of white Iowa voters having a favorable opinion of Hillary Clinton. Due to the small sample size of Iowa voters in the VOTER Survey and the inability to develop a full model of vote choice, a model examining the linkage between sexism and the 2016 election is not reported here. The basic model cited above is available from the author upon request.

2. Two major themes identified from the qualitative data in Chap. 2 were the enthusiasm gap and antipathy toward Hillary Clinton. Unfortunately, the Cooperative Congressional Election Survey did not include measures of favorability or excitement to vote for specific candidates. As a result, these themes cannot be tested at the individual level.

3. A detailed description of methodological approach to collecting the CCES is provided at http://cces.gov.harvard.edu.

4. All data analysis was performed using R and the CCES weight "common-weight_vv_post." Datasets with recodes, R scripts, and descriptives for the variables are available from the author upon request.

5. The "for all else" category only includes those respondents who provided a candidate's name for the survey item. It does not include self-reported nonvoters or respondents who refused to answer the question.

6. A vote switch variable was also constructed for Hillary Clinton, but only 11 Iowa respondents reported switching from Romney or a third-party candidate in 2012 to Clinton in 2016 preventing any analysis of vote switching toward Clinton.

7. The inclusion of the modern racism index is a better representation of racial attitudes based upon the narrative of vote switching in Iowa from 2012 to 2016 (i.e., if Iowa voters are racially conservative then why would they have voted for a black candidate in 2008 and 2012?). The narrative is more about viewing the political world through a color-blind lens as opposed to measures of racial resentment which measure antipathy that whites hold toward blacks regarding perceptions of work ethic and entitlement (see Sears and Henry 2003).

8. The CCES does not have a battery of questions regarding economic policy preferences, only the retrospective and prospective assessments of economy. Although the dataset does include an item regarding the use of the military to destroy a terrorist camp, it does not include a comprehensive

battery for terrorism either. The dataset does include items about preferences regarding the U.S. response to the Syrian conflict which could be
used as a proxy for terrorism policy, but the items were not asked of the
entire sample so there is significant missing data in those items.

9. It was asserted in the epigraph at the beginning of this chapter that Iowans
are conservative on issues of race and immigration. Looking at the racial
attitudes and immigration measures confirms this; however, the differences
were not statistically significant. The average score on the racial attitudes
measure for all white CCES respondents was 0.351. For white Iowa
respondents it was 0.367 ($t = 1.67$, $p = 0.095$). The average score on the
immigration measure for all white CCES respondents was 0.535 and for
white Iowa respondents was 0.560 ($t = 1.59$, $p = 0.112$).

10. Each predictor is scaled from 0 to 1. See Sect. 4.1 for a substantive description of the numeric codes for each predictor. The Obama Disapproval and
Party ID measures were not included in Fig. 4.1 as they are categorical in
nature.

11. A model was run which included the gun rights and abortion measures.
The inclusion added no value to the model, the coefficients were not statistically significant, and the remainder of the model was stable compared
to the model reported in Table 4.2.

12. The model has a limited number of cases coded 1 on the dependent variable. "Trump Switchers" constituted about 9% of the cases, which in real
terms is approximately 41 cases in all. The small number of Trump
Switchers in the model prevented disaggregating the modeling by college
degree or by party identification to see if there were differences between
groups. Additionally, adding predictors to the model will have the effect of
disaggregating cases even more creating small cell sizes for certain combi-
nations of predictors and the dependent variable which will lead to elevated
standard errors for the coefficients. If statistically significant predictors are
identified even with the reduced sample size, the likelihood is very good
that the effect is real and generalizable to white Iowa voters.

REFERENCES

Abramowitz, Alan, and Jennifer McCoy. 2019. United States: Racial Resentment,
Negative Partisanship, and Polarization in Trump's America. *Annals of the
American Academy of Political and Social Science* 681 (1): 137–156. https://
doi.org/10.1177%2F0002716218811309.
Abramowitz, Alan I., and Steven Webster. 2016. The Rise of Negative Partisanship
and the Nationalization of U.S. Elections in the 21st Century. *Electoral Studies*
41: 12–22. https://doi.org/10.1016/j.electstud.2015.11.001.

Achen, Christopher H., and Larry M. Bartels. 2016. *Democracy for Realists: Why Elections Do Not Produce Responsive Government*. Princeton, NJ: Princeton University Press.

Ansolabehere, Stephen, and Brian F. Schaffner. 2017. *Cooperative Congressional Election Study, 2016: Common Content*. [Computer File] Release 2: August 4, 2017. Cambridge, MA: Harvard University [producer]. http://cces.gov.harvard.edu.

Bartels, Larry M. 1988. *Presidential Primaries and the Dynamics of Public Choice*. Princeton, NJ: Princeton University Press.

———. 2002. Beyond the Running Tally: Partisan Bias in Political Perceptions. *Political Behavior* 24 (2): 117–150. https://doi.org/10.1023/A:1021226224601.

Campbell, Angus, Philip E. Converse, Warren E. Miller, and Donald E. Stokes. 1960. *The American Voter*. New York: John Wiley & Sons.

Cramer, Katherine J. 2016. *The Politics of Resentment: Rural Consciousness in Wisconsin and the Rise of Scott Walker*. Chicago: University of Chicago Press.

Democracy Fund Voter Study Group (DFVSG). 2017. *Views of the Electorate Research Survey, December 2016*. [Computer File] Release 1: August 28, 2017. Washington, DC: Democracy Fund Voter Study Group [producer]. https://www.voterstudygroup.org/.

Exit Polls. 2016. Exit Polls: Iowa President. Last Modified November 23, 2016. https://www.cnn.com/election/2016/results/exit-polls/iowa/president.

Filindra, Alexandra, and Noah J. Kaplan. 2016. Racial Resentment and Whites' Gun Policy Preferences in Contemporary America. *Political Behavior* 38 (2): 255–275. https://doi.org/10.1007/s11109-015-9326-4.

Fiorina, Morris P. 1981. *Retrospective Voting in American National Elections*. New Haven, CT: Yale University Press.

Golshan, Tara. 2016. Read Donald Trump's Most Inflammatory Speech Yet on Muslims and Immigration. *Vox*, June 13. https://www.vox.com/2016/6/13/11925122/trump-orlando-foreign-policy-transcript.

Hetherington, Marc J. 1996. The Media's Role in Forming Voters' National Economic Evaluations in 1992. *American Journal of Political Science* 40 (2): 372–395. https://doi.org/10.2307/2111629.

Hibbs, Douglas A. 1987. *The American Political Economy: Macroeconomics and Electoral Politics*. Cambridge, MA: Harvard University Press.

Hooghe, Marc, and Ruth Dassonneville. 2018. Explaining the Trump Vote: The Effect of Racist Resentment and Anti-Immigrant Sentiments. *PS: Political Science & Politics* 51 (3): 528–534. https://doi.org/10.1017/S1049096518000367.

Iyengar, Shanto, and Sean J. Westwood. 2015. Fear and Loathing Across Party Lines: New Evidence on Group Polarization. *American Journal of Political Science* 59 (3): 690–707. https://doi.org/10.1111/ajps.12152.

Keith, Bruce E., David B. Magleby, Candice J. Nelson, Elizabeth Orr, Mark C. Westlye, and Raymond E. Wolfinger. 1992. *The Myth of the Independent Voter*. Berkeley, CA: University of California Press.

Key, V.O. 1966. *The Responsible Electorate: Rationality in Presidential Voting, 1936–1960*. Cambridge, MA: Harvard University Press.

Kinder, Donald R., and Roderick Kiewiet. 1981. Sociotropic Politics: The American Case. *British Journal of Political Science* 11 (2): 129–161. https://doi.org/10.1017/S0007123400002544.

Klar, Samara, and Yanna Krupnikov. 2016. *Independent Politics: How American Disdain for Parties Leads to Political Inaction*. New York: Cambridge University Press.

Knuckey, Jonathan, and Myunghee Kim. 2015. Racial Resentment, Old-Fashioned Racism, and the Vote Choice of Southern and Nonsouthern Whites in the 2012 U.S. Presidential Election. *Social Science Quarterly* 96 (4): 905–922. https://doi.org/10.1111/ssqu.12184.

Lewis, Nicole. 2017. Comparing the 'Trump Economy' to the 'Obama Economy.' *Fact Checker Analysis, Washington Post*, December 14. https://www.washingtonpost.com/news/fact-checker/wp/2017/12/14/comparing-the-trump-economy-to-the-obama-economy/.

Lind, Dara. 2019. 'Immigrants are Coming Over the Border to Kill You' is the Only Speech Trump Knows How to Give. *Vox*, January 9. https://www.vox.com/2019/1/8/18174782/trump-speech-immigration-border.

Magleby, David B., Candice J. Nelson, and Mark C. Westlye. 2011. The Myth of the Independent Voter Revisited. In *Facing the Challenge of Democracy: Explorations in the Analysis of Public Opinion and Political Participation*, ed. Paul M. Sniderman and Benjamin Highton, 238–263. Princeton, NJ: Princeton University Press.

McElwee, Sean, and Jason McDaniel. 2017. Economic Anxiety Didn't Make People Vote for Trump, Racism Did. *Nation*, May 8. https://www.thenation.com/article/economic-anxiety-didnt-make-people-vote-trump-racism-did/.

McKee, Seth C., Daniel A. Smith, and M.V. (Trey) Hood III. 2019. The Comeback Kid: Donald Trump on Election Day in 2016. *PS: Political Science and Politics* 52 (2): 239–242. https://doi.org/10.1017/S1049096518001622.

McThomas, Mary, and Michael Tesler. 2016. The Growing Influence of Gender Attitudes on Public Support for Hillary Clinton, 2008–2012. *Politics & Gender* 12 (1): 28–49. https://doi.org/10.1017/S1743923X15000562.

Miller, Warren E., and J. Merrill Shanks. 1996. *The New American Voter*. Cambridge, MA: Harvard University Press.

Neville, Helen A., Roderick L. Lilly, Georgia Duran, Richard M. Lee, and LaVonne Browne. 2000. Construction and Initial Validation of the Color-Blind Racial Attitudes Scale (CoBRAS). *Journal of Counseling Psychology* 47 (1): 59–70. https://psycnet.apa.org/doi/10.1037/0022-0167.47.1.59.

Nowrasteh, Alex. 2018. The White House's Misleading & Error Ridden Narrative on Immigrants and Crime. *Cato at Liberty* (blog), *Cato Institute*, June 25. https://www.cato.org/blog/white-houses-misleading-error-ridden-narrative-immigrants-crime.

Piston, Spencer. 2010. How Explicit Racial Prejudice Hurt Obama in the 2008 Election. *Political Behavior* 32 (4): 431–451. https://doi.org/10.1007/s11109-010-9108-y.

Popkin, Samuel L. 1994. *The Reasoning Voter: Communication and Persuasion in Presidential Campaigns.* 2nd ed. Chicago: University of Chicago Press.

Reny, Tyler T., Loren Collingwood, and Ali A. Valenzuela. 2019. Vote Switching in the 2016 Election: How Racial and Immigration Attitudes, Not Economics, Explain Shifts in White Voting. *Public Opinion Quarterly* 83 (1): 91–113. https://doi.org/10.1093/poq/nfz011.

Schaffner, Brian F., Matthew MacWilliams, and Tatishe Nteta. 2018. Understanding White Polarization in the 2016 Vote for President: The Sobering Role of Racism and Sexism. *Political Science Quarterly* 133 (1): 9–34. https://doi.org/10.1002/polq.12737.

Sears, David O., and P.J. Henry. 2003. The Origins of Symbolic Racism. *Journal of Personality and Social Psychology* 85 (2): 259–275. https://psycnet.apa.org/doi/10.1037/0022-3514.85.2.259.

Setzler, Mark, and Alixandra B. Yanus. 2018. Why Did Women Vote for Donald Trump? *PS: Political Science & Politics* 51 (3): 523–527. https://doi.org/10.1017/S1049096518000355.

Sides, John, Michael Tesler, and Lynn Vavreck. 2018. *Identity Crisis: The 2016 Presidential Campaign and the Battle for the Meaning of America.* Princeton, NJ: Princeton University Press.

Tesler, Michael. 2012. The Spillover of Racialization into Health Care: How President Obama Polarized Public Opinion by Racial Attitudes and Race. *American Journal of Political Science* 56 (3): 690–704. https://doi.org/10.1111/j.1540-5907.2011.00577.x.

Valentino, Nicholas A., Carly Wayne, and Marzia Oceno. 2018a. Mobilizing Sexism: The Interaction of Emotion and Gender Attitudes in the 2016 US Presidential Election. *Public Opinion Quarterly* 82 (S1): 799–821. https://doi.org/10.1093/poq/nfy003.

Valentino, Nicholas A., Fabian G. Neuner, and L. Matthew Vandenbroek. 2018b. The Changing Norms of Racial Political Rhetoric and the End of Racial Priming. *Journal of Politics* 80 (3): 757–771. https://doi.org/10.1086/694845.

Wuthnow, Robert. 2018. *The Left Behind: Decline and Rage in Rural America.* Princeton, NJ: Princeton University Press.

CHAPTER 5

How Does 2016 Inform 2020 in Iowa?

*I think there's a potential for a very, very solid victory and not a whole
lot of drama leading up to that. I also see a scenario where, I don't see a
scenario at this point where he [Donald Trump] loses Iowa, I do see a
scenario where it's a smaller victory, and of course so much of that
depends on what happens on the outside.*
—Jeff Kaufmann, *Chairman of the Republican Party of Iowa*

Abstract In this chapter, I summarize the major findings of this book and
place them in the context of the academic literature on past presidential
elections, Iowa elections, and the 2016 presidential election. A discussion
of this book's major implications for the literature is also presented. This
chapter concludes with a discussion regarding what we can expect to see
as the 2020 election cycle continues.

Keywords Swing state • Immigration • Invisible primary • Iowa
Caucuses • Rural and urban counties

It has been nearly four years since Donald Trump came down the escalator
at Trump Tower to announce his candidacy for president. In that time, he
finished second in the Iowa Republican Caucus, defeated 16 candidates to
clinch the Republican nomination, and won the presidency by virtue of

© The Author(s) 2020   121
A. D. Green, *From the Iowa Caucuses to the White House*,
Palgrave Studies in US Elections,
https://doi.org/10.1007/978-3-030-22499-8_5

winning a majority of the vote in the Electoral College. As 2020 approaches and the primary and caucus season begins, Iowa voters will once again be asked to evaluate the candidate field across both parties. Even as the field on the Democratic side shapes up, many questions remain unanswered for political observers. Will President Trump have a serious caucus challenge in Iowa? How will Iowa Democrats evaluate the large field on the Democratic side? How will the new caucus rules proposed by the Iowa Democratic Party shape voter turnout and candidate selection? For many political scientists, the question becomes how will our understanding of the 2016 election inform what we observe during the 2020 cycle, particularly here in Iowa?

The focus of this project was to understand how Donald Trump, a thrice-married, billionaire businessman from Manhattan could come to Iowa and build a winning coalition of voters in 2016. Trump nearly won the Iowa Caucuses, finishing a close second but used the momentum built here to eventually catapult himself to the nomination. When he returned in late July 2016, Iowa voters continued attending his rallies in city after city. The crowds were diverse: There were Republican base voters, evangelical Christians, and white, working-class voters who came into the coalition due to Trump's positions on economic growth, trade, and immigration. The movement of white, working-class voters from the Obama coalition, while not a new trend in 2016, improved Trump's chances of winning Iowa's six Electoral College votes. On Election Day, Trump's supporters turned out in significant numbers, and Trump won the state by nearly 10%.

The qualitative and quantitative evidence presented throughout the last three chapters reveals Trump really was the perfect candidate at the perfect time in Iowa. The electorate, who had helped propel Barack Obama to the presidency in 2008 and again in 2012, was seeking change at the federal level. Iowa Republicans were certainly looking for change. They wanted to end Obamacare, minimize the regulatory burden on business and industry, and pursue a different path on immigration. White, working-class voters sought change through Obama's candidacy in 2008 and 2012. By 2016, when the economic recovery had not yet reached the working-class and rural areas of the state, they sought change through an "outsider" candidate named Donald Trump. The qualitative evidence indicates that some working-class Democrats not only voted for Trump, but they even changed their party identification, canvassed, and put campaign-provided or homemade Trump signs in their yard or fence line. They also spoke with friends, family, and neighbors about Trump's candidacy. It was a rejection of the establishment in Washington, a continuation of the populist trend that has shaped Iowa politics for generations.

Trump's candidacy came at a time when establishment politicians were running for office in both parties. Trump defeated 15 of the 16 Republican candidates vying for the nomination in the Iowa Caucuses, including establishment figures like Jeb Bush, Marco Rubio, John Kasich, and Chris Christie. Then, once he secured the nomination, he faced a quintessential insider manifested by Hillary Clinton. As the evidence in Chap. 2 suggests, Clinton's experience as a U.S. Senator and Secretary of State could not offset her "negatives." Trump's "Crooked Hillary" narrative resonated with Iowa voters in both parties and among No Party voters. Thus, in an election when voters wanted change for a variety of reasons, electing an insider candidate was not an option.

Economic issues certainly were important to Iowa voters in 2016, but other issues were important to Trump voters as well. As the evidence in Chap. 4 shows, gun rights, abortion, and immigration were all viewed by county party officials as important issues to Trump voters. Still, no issue shaped support for Trump like the battery of policy positions on immigration. Iowa voters with hardline positions on immigration policy were much more likely to support Trump in 2016, regardless of their party affiliation. Democrats with the most hardline positions on immigration were almost 8% more likely to vote for Trump than Republicans with the most pro-immigration attitudes. Furthermore, the effect of immigration attitudes on supporting Trump was stronger for white, college-educated voters than it was for white, working-class voters. Some may be surprised that immigration was such an important factor in 2016 in Iowa. Iowa is not a border state and has a homogeneous population. However, immigration has been a significant political issue dating back to the late 1990s as the Hispanic population grew. In 2000, Governor Tom Vilsack's efforts to define Iowa as an "immigrant enterprise zone" were publicly rejected by white Iowans (Lay 2012, 16). Two years later, Vilsack, a Democrat, would sign a bill making English the state's official language. The results suggest understanding the issue of immigration is vital to understanding election results in Iowa, at least when voters are primed to view the election through the lens of immigration and race (e.g., Sides et al. 2018).

Racial attitudes mattered in 2016 as well. Iowa voters with racially conservative views were significantly more likely to disapprove of President Obama's performance, and they held more hardline positions on immigration, both of which were directly linked to support for Trump. More racially conservative positions, however, were directly linked to vote switching in 2016, or voting for Trump after supporting Obama or a third-party candidate in 2012. The effect of holding racially conservative attitudes on the chance of vote switching was strongest for Democrats and No Party voters, as Republicans were very unlikely to be vote switchers in 2016. As mentioned in the previous chapter, the finding does not suggest all Trump voters are racists. Rather, it reveals Trump switchers were more likely to deny that racism exists compared to those who supported Obama in 2012 and Hillary Clinton in 2016. Some may indeed be racists, but a sizable number of Trump switchers actually scored below the average on the racial attitudes index, suggesting other factors shaped their decision to cast a vote for Trump in 2016 after supporting Obama or a third-party candidate in 2012.[1]

Finally, it is important to remember Iowa is a swing state. It is clear from the results presented in the previous three chapters that there is a cohort of voters in Iowa who are willing to shift between candidates from the two major parties, based upon contextual factors that vary from campaign to campaign. Not only did we see this phenomenon in 2016, but also in the 2018 midterm election, when Governor Kim Reynolds was elected to her first full term on the same ballot where two Republican incumbents were defeated in their re-election bids for the U.S. House, and a third was nearly defeated. There is no doubt some Democrats and some Republicans are willing to occasionally defect from their party's candidate from time to time. However, the significant number of No Party voters in Iowa certainly shapes Iowa's swing state status as well. No Party voters made up more than a third of the electorate in 2016; according to data from the 2016 Cooperative Congressional Election Survey (CCES), 13.1% of white No Party voters were vote switchers in 2016 (Exit Polls 2016; Ansolabehere and Schaffner 2017). Additionally, about three-quarters of Trump switchers surveyed in the CCES indicated they had not participated in the Iowa Caucuses earlier in the year, corroborating accounts from state and local party leaders regarding an influx of new volunteers and voters after Trump's nomination. These new participants were more likely to be No Party voters (16.3%), but 14.9% were Democrats and 9% were Republicans. This finding suggests that understanding the political behavior of both No Party voters and infrequent voters is essential in explaining why Iowa is consistently a swing state. Future research should focus on these cohorts, especially considering that a comprehensive study of Iowa's No Party voters has not been completed to date.

Therefore, how do the results of 2016 inform what we can expect in Iowa during the 2020 Iowa Caucuses and the November 2020 general election? The remainder of this chapter focuses on key questions that political scientists and observers of Iowa politics are asking regarding candidates from both parties, and it provides answers grounded in the political science literature and publicly available data.

5.1   THE 2020 REPUBLICAN CAUCUS: WILL TRUMP HAVE A CHALLENGER?[2]

The main question on the Republican side is whether President Trump will have a serious caucus challenger come February 2020. While Republican challengers have made serious attempts to defeat incumbent Republican presidents in the past, most notably Pat Buchanan in 1992, potential Republican challengers to Trump are taking a very cautious approach to the 2020 cycle. Establishment Republican candidates such as Governor Larry Hogan of Maryland, as well as former Governor John Kasich of Ohio, have hinted at potential challenges (Stanage 2019). Former Massachusetts Governor Bill Weld formally declared his intention to challenge President Trump in April 2019. The question now becomes whether there is a path to a strong showing in the Iowa Caucuses, which could build momentum for the New Hampshire primary and beyond.

If a Republican challenger emerges, do not expect to see the candidate in Iowa. The reason? Trump is still very popular in Iowa with Republican voters. According to a recent March 2019 CNN/*Des Moines Register*/Mediacom Iowa Poll, Trump's approval rating among Iowa Republicans is 81% and his favorability rating is 82% (Agiesta 2019). While 40% of Iowa Republicans are hoping for a challenger to emerge, 67% of Iowa Republicans are certain they will vote for Trump in November 2020. Additionally, most of the state political elites interviewed for this project do not anticipate a strong caucus challenger to emerge in Iowa. When you couple this knowledge with the Republican elite support Trump enjoys as discussed in Chap. 2, one finds a state which provides a formidable political challenge for anyone entering the caucus against Trump. Potential candidates such as Hogan, Kasich, or Weld may find a more favorable electorate in Republican primary contests further into the calendar year, including in New Hampshire. That being said, Trump will more than likely not face a strong challenge nationwide either. His approval rating among likely Republican primary voters and caucus participants currently sits at 85% (Morning Consult 2019). For candidates who are considering a run, it may make more sense to sit 2020 out and run in 2024, when the Republican nomination will be up for grabs again.

5.2   The 2020 Democratic Caucus: Making Sense of a Crowded Field

The picture on the Democratic side is not as clear. Two real questions emerge when thinking about the winner of the 2020 Iowa Democratic Caucus: (1) Will the winner of the "invisible primary" be the winner on caucus night?; and (2) What effect will caucus reforms have on the outcome?

With such a large field, it is hard to fathom Iowa Democrats will play the role of "king-maker" in February 2020. Democratic Caucus-goers will be asked to "winnow the field," or narrow the range of options for Democrats in other states (Squire 2008). Even though Iowa's role is to shape the field, it is important for candidates to have a good showing here. Neither frontrunners nor candidates from the middle of the pack or lower can afford to underperform in Iowa, and candidates who overperform are oftentimes rewarded in future states. Candidates finishing outside of the top quarter of this cycle's field will seriously have to consider moving on to New Hampshire. Strong performers are usually rewarded with media coverage, which helps shape results in New Hampshire and beyond (Winebrenner and Goldford 2010; Redlawsk et al. 2011; Donovan et al. 2014).

Up until the fourth week of April 2019, 20 candidates had announced their intentions to run for the Democratic nomination, with five additional Democrats still considering a run (NYT 2019). Polling from March 2019 showed that former Vice President Joe Biden and Vermont Senator Bernie Sanders were leading the Democratic field, with approximately a quarter of Iowa Democrats supporting each candidate (Emerson 2019; Enten 2019). As Harry Enten indicates, polling data this early in the campaign is driven significantly by name recognition, so it is not surprising that Biden and Sanders would be leading the Iowa field this early in the contest. As Iowa voters become more familiar with the other 18 candidates, the expectation becomes that several candidates will see their favorability and preference share increase.

Now, how will the Democratic candidates improve their name recognition with Iowa voters in hopes of exceeding the 15% viability threshold in the caucuses? The candidates are currently part of what political scientists call "the invisible primary," where they raise money and make visits to early states to court voters and seek out elite support to sell voters on their "viability" (i.e., can the candidate win the nomination?) and "electability" (i.e., can the candidate win the general election?) (Redlawsk et al. 2011; Masket 2019). While money does not always determine the outcome of primary elections, money is important indeed. Candidates must anticipate the cost of financing a winning operation in the nomination stage, including the financing of state visits, staff salaries, get-out-the-vote efforts, traditional advertising, and digital operations (Ezra 2004). Financing is not only a sign of strength for Iowa Caucus candidates, it can also signal strength to voters down the political road. The 2020 cycle is no different. As of early April 2019, seven Democratic candidates had released their first-quarter fundraising totals publicly (Breuninger and Schoen 2019). Leading the way was Bernie Sanders with $18.2 million, followed by California Senator Kamala Harris at $12 million. Former U.S. Representative Beto O'Rourke was third on the list with $9.4 million raised, which is an amazing figure considering that O'Rourke had been in the race for less than a month. Rounding out the top seven were Minnesota Senator Amy Klobuchar ($5.2 million), New Jersey Senator Corey Booker ($5 million), and entrepreneur Andrew Yang ($1.7 million). Candidates near the top of the list will inevitably have enough funds to maintain a significant presence in Iowa throughout the caucus season, and they will still have ample funding for other early states.

Campaign visits matter as well. By visiting early states, candidates can court voters and build momentum for their candidacy. As previously mentioned, early polling in the horserace is significantly shaped by name recognition (Enten 2019), so the act of getting in front of voters is important. Visits to Iowa during the caucuses are vital to candidates. Research on the Iowa Caucuses by Christopher Hull (2008) reveals that the more days a candidate is in the state, the higher his or her vote share will be. Iowa voters not only expect to see the candidates during campaigns, they also expect to have access to the candidates to pose questions about the campaign (Larimer 2015). According to visit data aggregated by the *Des Moines Register* (2019), the first potential Democratic candidate to visit Iowa was former Missouri Secretary of State Jason Kander in December 2016. From the day after the November 2016 election through April 10, 2019, 34 potential candidates for the Democratic nomination had visited 93 of Iowa's 99 counties. In doing so, candidates have made appearances at 578 events since November 9, 2016. Many of the events were attended by former Representative John Delaney from Maryland, who has made appearances at 137 events in 88 counties, indicative of his need to build name recognition in the state. Polling from March 2019 showed that 61% of likely Democratic Caucus participants did not have enough information about Delaney to make a favorability assessment of him (Iowa Poll 2019).

Figure 5.1 displays the number of candidates who have visited each Iowa county since November 9, 2016. In the figure, the darker shades of gray represent a larger number of candidates who have visited the county. Three trends stand out. One, Democratic candidates are visiting Democratic strongholds that Hillary Clinton won in 2016 (Black Hawk, Johnson, Linn, Polk, Scott, and Story Counties) more so than rural counties, suggesting an emphasis on building networks in those counties. Two, notice the shade of gray for Dubuque County in northeast Iowa and Woodbury County in northwest Iowa. Fourteen Democratic candidates have attended 25 events in Woodbury County, and 11 candidates have attended 13 events in Dubuque County. Both counties were pivot counties in 2016 and will be must-wins in 2020, if the Democratic nominee

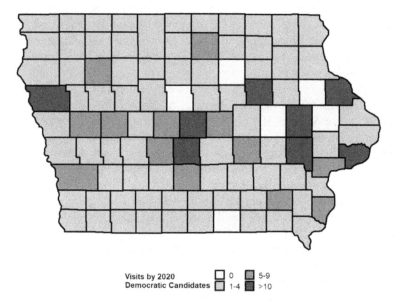

Visits by 2020
Democratic Candidates
☐ 0   ▨ 5-9
☐ 1-4 ■ >10

Fig. 5.1 Visits to Iowa counties by potential 2020 Democratic candidates. Map data from "maps" and "mapdata" packages in R

wants to win the state. A higher number of candidates visiting both counties suggest strategic targeting of both counties. Three, notice the darker shades of gray around Polk County, home of the Des Moines metro. Warren County to the south and Dallas County to the west are rapidly suburbanizing. The fact that candidates are focusing on these areas could be evidence of an emphasis on courting college-educated voters in the suburbs around Des Moines, which will be important not only during the caucuses but also in November 2020.

Endorsements also matter because they transmit important information to voters in elections (Miller and Shanks 1996). When political elites signal their support for a candidate through a formal endorsement, it sends an important message to fellow party members that the candidate is worth supporting. In a way, the political elite is "vouching" for the candidate with the voters. In Chap. 2, the importance of elite support in 2016 was discussed. Donald Trump enjoyed significant support from Iowa's Republican elite, which helped fortify the winning coalition he built. In the 2020 cycle, endorsements are slowly starting to appear for Democratic candidates intending to run in the Iowa Caucuses. As of the end of February 2019, six Democratic candidates held endorsements from Iowa Democrats, including Senator Corey Booker, Representative John Delaney, Representative Tulsi Gabbard (HI), Senator Kamala Harris, and Senator Amy Klobuchar (ISL 2019). Most of the endorsements come from local and regional endorsers, but two prominent names stand out on the list. First, Deidre DeJear, the 2018 Democratic nominee for Iowa Secretary of State, is serving as the campaign chair for Harris. Second, Andy McGuire, former candidate for governor and chairwoman of the Iowa Democratic Party (IDP), is serving as the campaign chair for Klobuchar. The real question as we move toward February 2020 is whether or not endorsements will be made by former Senator Tom Harkin, former Governors Tom Vilsack or Chet Culver, or current U.S. Representatives Abby Finkenauer, Dave Loebsack, or Cindy Axne. Endorsements from the aforementioned individuals would be an important cue for Democratic Caucus participants and could push a candidate over the 15% viability threshold.

Another key question on the Democratic side becomes what effect will the rules changes proposed by the IDP have on the 2020 Democratic Caucus? In the aftermath of 2016, the IDP began investigating reforms which would increase caucus accessibility and transparency (Hermann 2019). In February 2019, the IDP released a proposal of five reforms to the caucus process.[3] Of the five, one of the reforms could have a noticeable impact on the outcome of the caucuses. For the first time, Iowa Democrats will have the option of participating in a "virtual caucus" via phone or electronic device. Voters will "preference rank" up to five candidates, and 10% of the delegate count will be linked to the outcomes of the virtual caucuses. By doing so, Iowa Democrats who cannot attend a traditional caucus site will be able to participate in the caucus process. This new option could increase the turnout of younger Iowans, who are generally more mobile and may be away from their home precinct on caucus night. It could also increase the turnout of older Iowans, who are not capable of attending a traditional caucus or may be snowbirds during the winter months (McCormick 2019). The effects of the reform will not only impact turnout but will also impact candidate strategy. During the 2020 cycle, candidates will be required to mobilize caucus participants at traditional sites and in the virtual caucuses, as the 10% delegate allocation is too sizable for candidates to ignore.

5.3   The 2020 General Election: Another Iowa Swing?

In January 2019, the Cook Political Report (2019) identified Iowa as a "Lean Republican" state for the 2020 election cycle. As the epigraph at the beginning of this chapter outlines, President Trump will be considered the frontrunner in Iowa going into the 2020 cycle. Even though his overall approval rating is underwater by 10%, Trump is still very popular among Iowa Republicans (Agiesta 2019; Morning Consult 2019), and his organization will certainly attempt to build upon the gains made by Republicans in both 2016 and in 2018. As Harry Enten (2018) argues, however, "Trump does not walk on political water. He does not defy political gravity." If his national favorability ratings remain stable, he will enter the general election as "the least popular president to run for reelection in the history of polling" (Bitecofer and Kidd 2019). While Trump may be in a good position across the state, he is not invincible. Iowa will have the cohort of "change" voters who swing from election to election, and their loyalty could be up for grabs again in 2020. As Jeff Kaufmann (2019) alludes to in the epigraph, there are some "outside" factors that could trim the margin from what it was in 2016 to coming within striking distance for the Democratic nominee in 2020. Therefore, if Iowa is going to pivot back to Democratic blue, three things must happen.

First, candidate selection will be everything. Even though Trump's favorability rating in 2016 was the worst on record, Trump was able to leverage Hillary Clinton's negatives to his advantage. 2016 became the year about the "lesser of two evils," and Trump came out on top (Enten 2018). For Democrats, it is essential to select a nominee who can withstand the attacks that will inevitably come from Trump's campaign. If Democrats select a nominee with significant negatives or vulnerability, it could give Trump the same advantage he had over Clinton, allowing him to frame the campaign on the same terms. The perceived ideological position of the Democratic nominee could matter as well. The President is testing election messages, which label Democrats as socialists who are "out of touch radicals" (Cook and Restuccia 2019). His campaign team believes that pinning such a label on the Democratic nominee is a winning strategy, similar to how the campaign pinned the label "Crooked Hillary" on Clinton, which hurt her electability in 2016. The selection of a nominee who could be pinned with the label of "socialist" could hurt Democratic attempts to win back No Party voters and Democrats who vote-switched in 2016. As a result, Democratic Caucus participants need to pay attention to the "electability" of the candidate. There is evidence Iowa Democrats are thinking about electability. In polling data from March 2019, the two frontrunners for the Democratic nomination, Joe Biden and Bernie Sanders, led Trump in hypothetical head-to-head matchups by 6% and 2%, respectively (Emerson 2019). Additionally, 44% of likely caucus participants view Bernie Sanders as "too liberal," and 33% would be dissatisfied if "the Democratic Party nominated someone who thinks the country should be more socialist" (Iowa Poll 2019). Electability will matter in 2020, and an "electable" Democratic nominee could resonate across Iowa.

The selection of the perfect nominee is also instrumental in winning back votes in eastern Iowa. As discussed in the opening chapter, Democrats have voter registration advantages in eastern Iowa; but, in 2016, Trump was able to win counties that had not been won by Republicans in decades (Cohen and Simon 2016). Finding a candidate who brings a message that resonates not only with Democratic voters in urban areas across Iowa but also throughout more rural eastern Iowa counties could go a long way in winning back voters who chose Barack Obama in 2008 and 2012. This strategic approach is particularly important for reaching white, working-class Democrats, who tend to fall right-of-center on issues such as immigration and government regulation (Freedlander 2018). By doing so, the nominee would be in a better position to return vote shares to Obama 2012 levels in the major urban areas of the state, yet he or she could improve upon Hillary Clinton's performance in some eastern Iowa rural counties, which should narrow the margin between the nominee and Trump. The Democratic nominee for governor in 2018, Fred Hubbell, was able to win five eastern Iowa counties that Trump won two years prior (Clinton, Des Moines, Dubuque, Jefferson, and Lee Counties). The Democratic nominee for president needs to build upon those gains to defeat Trump statewide in 2020.

Finally, Democrats need to focus on rural Iowa. As discussed in Chap. 2, many respondents to the survey of county party officials highlighted the lack of outreach and messaging toward rural Iowa from the Clinton campaign. Whether this neglect was intentional (i.e., the Clinton campaign knew it could not win rural Iowa) or unintentional (i.e., the strategic messaging focused on identity and issues more salient to urban Democrats) remains unsettled. Either way, it resulted in rural Iowa voters who felt ignored and left behind by the Democratic Party. Based upon interviews with state political elites, some agreed there were rural voters available to be courted by the Clinton campaign, if an appropriate message had been effectively delivered. Others were not so sure. Regardless, Democrats must perform better in rural Iowa in 2020 if they want to win the state. As one Democratic respondent to the survey of party officials from southeast Iowa said, "Democrats will need to learn to better explain how their policies and social positions are beneficial to rural Iowans. 2016 and 2018 both showed that relying on the urban counties to carry elections for Democrats is no longer a viable strategy." Some have argued that the nomination of a midwestern candidate, like Amy Klobuchar from Minnesota, who has built coalitions of rural and urban voters in the past, may be the best path forward to win states like Iowa (Kaul 2019). Regardless of who the nominee will be, the candidate must be comfortable campaigning in both rural and urban counties, and he or she must have a message that resonates with the concerns of rural Iowans, such as agriculture and trade, jobs, infrastructure, and even immigration. Immigration was a salient issue that shaped the Iowa vote for Trump in 2016, and the President seems ready and willing to use immigration as an electoral wedge again in 2020 (Shear and Ember 2019). Leonard and Russell (2019) argue, "Democrats have an opportunity to put forward a smart approach to immigration" because "manufacturers and farm operators need workers." If the nominee can succeed in shaping a message on salient issues, including immigration, that resonates in rural Iowa, rural

Obama supporters from 2008 and 2012, who shifted to Trump in 2016, might be willing to swing back toward the Democratic candidate in 2016. In the end, the Democratic nominee does not need to win the rural vote in 2020. Obama lost the rural vote in Iowa by 6% in 2012 (Exit Polls 2012). However, the 2020 nominee cannot lose the rural vote by 30%, as Clinton did, and expect to win Iowa (Exit Polls 2016).

NOTES

1. Some readers may wonder about the impact of the Comey Letter to Congress on October 28, 2016, or the impact of Russian interference on Iowa voters in 2016. While it is certainly plausible the Comey Letter or Russian interference could have impacted the vote choices of Iowa voters, it is hard to imagine that either was determinative considering the final margin in Iowa between Trump and Clinton was 9.5%. Furthermore, quantifying the impact of either would be difficult in statistical models of vote choice, so neither was analyzed in this volume. For more analysis on the impact of the Comey Letter or Russian interference, see Silver (2017) or Sides et al. (2018).
2. The Mueller Report was publicly released by the U.S. Department of Justice on April 18, 2019, approximately two weeks before this book manuscript was finalized. The full impact of the Mueller Report on 2020 is yet unknown.
3. At the time this chapter was written, the IDP proposals had not yet been approved by the Democratic National Committee.

REFERENCES

Agiesta, Jennifer. 2019. Iowa Poll: Trump Remains Strong Among Iowa Republicans, But Some Hope for a Challenger. *CNN*, March 11. https://www.cnn.com/2019/03/11/politics/cnn-poll-iowa-republicans-trump/index.html.

Ansolabehere, Stephen, and Brian F. Schaffner. 2017. *Cooperative Congressional Election Study, 2016: Common Content.* [Computer File] Release 2: August 4, 2017. Cambridge, MA: Harvard University [producer]. http://cces.gov.harvard.edu.

Bitecofer, Rachel, and Quentin Kidd. 2019. National Survey of 2020 Likely Voters. The Judy Ford Wason Center for Public Policy, Christopher Newport University, February 26. http://wasoncenter.cnu.edu/wp-content/uploads/2019/04/Wason-Center-2020-National-Survey-Report-Final.pdf.

Breuninger, Kevin, and John W. Schoen. 2019. Here's What the 2020 Democratic Candidates Say They've Raised in the First Quarter. *CNBC*, April 3. https://www.cnbc.com/2019/04/03/heres-what-the-2020-democratic-candidates-raised-in-the-first-quarter.html.

Cohen, Marshall, and Jeff Simon. 2016. How Democrats Lost Dubuque, and Middle America. *CNNPolitics*, December 14. https://www.cnn.com/2016/12/14/politics/democrats-lost-dubuque-middle-america/index.html.

Cook Political Report. 2019. The Cook Political Report: 2020 Electoral College Ratings. Accessed April 10, 2019. https://www.cookpolitical.com/sites/default/files/2019-01/EC.pdf.

Cook, Nancy, and Andrew Restuccia. 2019. 'High-Level Fear-Mongering': Trump's Economic Team Drives 'Socialism' Attack. *Politico*, March 20. https://www.politico.com/story/2019/03/20/white-house-economic-2020-socialism-1228725.

Des Moines Register. 2019. Candidate Tracker. *Des Moines Register*. Accessed April 9, 2019. http://data.desmoinesregister.com/iowa-caucus/candidate-tracker/index.php.

Donovan, Todd, David Redlawsk, and Caroline Tolbert. 2014. The 2012 Iowa Republican Caucus and Its Effects on the Presidential Nomination Contest. *Presidential Studies Quarterly* 44 (3): 447–466.

Emerson. 2019. Iowa 2020: Biden and Sanders Neck and Neck in Democratic Field, Mayor Pete Jumps to Double Digits. *Emerson College Poll*, March 24. https://emersonpolling.reportablenews.com/pr/iowa-2020-biden-and-sanders-neck-and-neck-in-democratic-field-mayor-pete-jumps-to-double-digits.

Enten, Harry. 2018. The Midterms Show Trump Does Not Defy Political Gravity. *CNN*, November 10. https://www.cnn.com/2018/11/10/politics/poll-of-the-week-trump-no-defying-gravity/index.html.

———. 2019. Name Recognition Is Key and Four Other Takeaways from Our Iowa Poll. *CNN*, March 11. https://www.cnn.com/2019/03/11/politics/enten-iowa-poll-recognition-takeaways/index.html.

Exit Polls. 2012. Exit Polls: Iowa President. Last Modified December 10. http://www.cnn.com/election/2012/results/state/IA/president/.

———. 2016. Exit Polls: Iowa President. Last Modified November 23. https://www.cnn.com/election/2016/results/exit-polls/iowa/president.

Ezra, Marni. 2004. Candidate Nominations and General Election Strategy. In *Campaigns and Elections: American Style*, ed. James A. Thurber and Candice J. Nelson, 57–66. Boulder, CO: Westview Press.

Freedlander, David. 2018. The Democrats' Culture Divide. *Politico Magazine*, November/December. https://www.politico.com/magazine/story/2018/10/30/democratic-party-culture-divide-wars-working-class-blue-collar-221913.

Hermann, Jonah. 2019. Iowa Democratic Party Proposes Historic Changes to 2020 Iowa Caucuses. *Iowa Democratic Party*, February 11. https://iowademocrats.org/iowa-democratic-party-proposes-historic-changes-2020-iowa-caucuses/.

Hull, Christopher C. 2008. *Grassroots Rules: How the Iowa Caucus Helps Elect American Presidents*. Stanford: Stanford University Press.

Iowa Poll. 2019. CNN/*Des Moines Register*/Mediacom Iowa Poll: March 3–6, 2019. Accessed April 9, 2019. http://cdn.cnn.com/cnn/2019/images/03/09/rel1_ia1.pdf.

Iowa Starting Line (ISL). 2019. 2020 Endorsements. *Iowa Starting Line.* Last Modified February 26, 2019. https://iowastartingline.com/2020-endorsements/.

Kaufmann, Jeff. 2019. Interview by Author. *Des Moines*, February 14.

Kaul, Greta. 2019. Amy Klobuchar May Be Minnesota's Most Popular Politician. But How Popular Is She in Minnesota's Trump Country? *MinnPost*, February 14. https://www.minnpost.com/national/2019/02/amy-klobuchar-may-be-minnesotas-most-popular-politician-but-how-popular-is-she-in-minnesotas-trump-country/.

Larimer, Christopher W. 2015. *Gubernatorial Stability in Iowa: A Stranglehold on Power.* New York: Palgrave Macmillan.

Lay, J. Celeste. 2012. *A Midwestern Mosaic: Immigration and Political Socialization in Rural America.* Philadelphia: Temple University Press.

Leonard, Robert, and Matt Russell. 2019. What Democrats Need to Know to Win in Rural America. *New York Times*, March 17. https://www.nytimes.com/2019/03/17/opinion/democrats-iowa-caucus.html.

Masket, Seth. 2019. The 2020 Invisible Primary in Light of 2016. *Mischiefs of Faction* (blog), *Vox*, January 7. https://www.vox.com/mischiefs-of-faction/2019/1/7/18170894/2020-invisible-primary-2016-democrats.

McCormick, John. 2019. 'Virtual Caucuses' Could Skew Iowa's 2020 Electorate Even Older. *Bloomberg*, April 3. https://www.bloomberg.com/news/articles/2019-04-03/-virtual-caucuses-could-skew-iowa-s-2020-electorate-even-older.

Miller, Warren E., and J. Merrill Shanks. 1996. *The New American Voter.* Cambridge, MA: Harvard University Press.

Morning Consult. 2019. Tracking Trump: The President's Standing Across America. *Morning Consult.* Last Modified April 5, 2019. https://morningconsult.com/tracking-trump/.

New York Times (NYT). 2019. Who's Running for President in 2020? *New York Times.* Accessed April 9, 2019. https://www.nytimes.com/interactive/2019/us/politics/2020-presidential-candidates.html.

Redlawsk, David P., Caroline J. Tolbert, and Todd Donovan. 2011. *Why Iowa? How Caucuses and Sequential Elections Improve the Presidential Nominating Process.* Chicago: University of Chicago Press.

Shear, Michael D., and Sydney Ember. 2019. 'Dangerous People are Coming Here and the Good People are Dying,' Trump Warns in Texas Visit. *New York Times*, April 10. https://www.nytimes.com/2019/04/10/us/politics/trump-texas-crosby.html.

Sides, John, Michael Tesler, and Lynn Vavreck. 2018. *Identity Crisis: The 2016 Presidential Campaign and the Battle for the Meaning of America.* Princeton, NJ: Princeton University Press.

Silver, Nate. 2017. The Comey Letter Probably Cost Clinton the Election. *FiveThirtyEight.com*, May 3. https://fivethirtyeight.com/features/the-comey-letter-probably-cost-clinton-the-election/.

Squire, Peverill. 2008. The Iowa Caucuses, 1972–2008: A Eulogy. *The Forum* 5 (4): 1–9. https://doi.org/10.2202/1540-8884.1212.

Stanage, Niall. 2019. Rough Road Awaits Trump Rival in GOP Primary. *The Memo* (blog), *The Hill*, March 19. https://thehill.com/homenews/the-memo/434637-the-memo-rough-road-awaits-any-trump-rival-in-gop-primary.

Winebrenner, Hugh, and Dennis J. Goldford. 2010. *The Iowa Precinct Caucuses: The Making of a Media Event.* 3rd ed. Iowa City: The University of Iowa Press.

INDEX[1]

A

ABC News/*Washington Post*, 24
Abortion, 71, 94
    predicting Trump support, 106
    voter issue, 101, 103, 110, 114
Access Hollywood tape, 30, 61
Affective partisanship, 60, 94
Affirmative action, 96
African Americans
    stereotypes about, 96
    voter turnout of, 65
Allamakee County, 9, 30
Amateurism, 5
American Voter, The (Campbell *et al*),
    59–60, 93, 94, 100
Asian Americans, voter
    turnout of, 65
Audubon County, 9
Axne, Cindy, 129

B

Benghazi attack, 32
Benton County, 9
Biden, Joe, 126, 131
Billy Graham Center Institute,
    Wheaton College, 71
Black Hawk County, 7, 11, 25, 26,
    58, 128
Blum, Rod, 42
Boeyink, Jeff, 23
    on antipathy toward Clinton, 35
    on campaign organization/elite
        support, 41–42
    on change voting, 48
    on enthusiasm gap, 24
    on rural-urban divide, 45–46
Booker, Corey, 127, 129
Boone County, 80
Boswell, Leonard, 43

[1] Note: Page numbers followed by 'n' refer to notes.

© The Author(s) 2020
A. D. Green, *From the Iowa Caucuses to the White House*,
Palgrave Studies in US Elections,
https://doi.org/10.1007/978-3-030-22499-8

Preibus, Reince, 40, 41
Price, Troy, 23
    on antipathy toward Clinton, 32
    on campaign organization/elite
        support, 36, 37
    on enthusiasm gap, 25
    on rural-urban divide, 45
Pro-Life Iowans for Trump, 41

Q
Qualitative methodology, 20–21
    interviews, 22
    methods and data, 21–24
    questionnaire, 21
    survey, 21–22

R
Race and identity, in 2016 campaign,
    65–67
Racial attitudes
    election issue, 123, 124
    immigration and, 92–94
    likelihood of vote switching and,
        108, 111, 112
    predicting Trump support, 106, 111
Racism, 50, 51, 92, 93, 97, 98
Reagan, Ronald, 71
Registered voters, Iowa, 5
Republican Caucus (2020), challenge
    to Trump, 125–126
Republican National Committee
    (RNC), 40–41
Republican National Convention
    (RNC), 2
Republican Party, 20, 23, 39, 71
    elite of, endorsing Trump, 61
    phone banks, 29
Republican voters, 77
    predicting pivot counties, 81
    predicting Trump support, 106, 111

Trump's overperformance of
    Romney, 78
    in western Iowa, 7, 15n2
Reynolds, Kim, 6, 50, 61, 124
Riff-raff, 96
Roast and Ride, Ernst's, 31, 42
Romney, Mitt, 9–10, 14
    Trump overperforming, 58, 59, 61,
        72, 76–82
    two-party vote share, 11, 12
Rubio, Marco, 2, 123
Rural areas, definition, 68
Rural consciousness, 68
Rural-Urban Continuum Code
    (RUCC), 69–70
Rural-urban divide, support for Trump
    and, 68–70
Russian interference in 2016 election,
    133n1

S
Sanders, Bernie, 23, 33, 34, 126, 131
    Democratic candidate (2020), 126
    fundraising, 127
    primary with Clinton, 34
    supporters of, 33, 35
"Scapegoating," 34
Scott County, 7, 11, 12, 58, 128
Second (2nd) Amendment, 2, 102
Sexism, 49–51, 92, 93, 97,
    114–115n1
Sioux County, 7, 73
Sociotropic assessment, 99, 100
Split-ticket voting, 5, 6
Springsteen, Bruce, 9
Star Wars analogy, 35
Stein, Jill, 12, 33
Story County, 11, 12, 58, 73, 128
Strain of populism, 20, 48
Supreme Court, 71
Swing state, 6, 124

W

Wapello County, 58

Warren County, 11, 129

Washington Post, The (newspaper), 9

Webster County, 79

Weld, Bill, 125

Wheaton College, 71

White, working-class voters
  predicting vote shifts, 79
    support for Trump, 61–64

Wisconsin, 68, 82

Woodbury County, 7, 9, 10, 79, 80, 128

"Wrong minded," 34

Y

Yang, Andrew, 127

Yard signs, Trump, 29–31

Young, David, 42

CPSIA information can be obtained
at www.ICGtesting.com
Printed in the USA
LVHW080027181019
634542LV00008B/232/P